Books Appeal to Teachers

Books Appeal to Teachers

*Getting Teachers
to Use the School Library
Across the Curriculum*

by

Karen Cornell Gomberg

McFarland & Company, Inc., Publishers
Jefferson, North Carolina, and London

British Library Cataloguing-in-Publication data are available

Library of Congress Cataloguing-in-Publication Data

Gomberg, Karen Cornell.
    Books appeal to teachers : getting teachers to use the school
library across the curriculum / by Karen Cornell Gomberg.
        p.   cm.
    Includes bibliographical references and index.
    ISBN 0-89950-490-6 (sewn softcover : 55# alk. paper) ∞
    1. Teachers—Library orientation.   2. Media programs (Education)
3. Libraries and education.   4. Libraries and teachers.
5. Curriculum planning.   6. School libraries.   I. Title.
Z711.2.G65   1990
025.5'6—dc20   90-52655
                                                                      CIP

Manufactured in the United States of America

McFarland & Company, Inc., Publishers
    Box 611, Jefferson, North Carolina 28640

This book is dedicated
to
my precious father, William Lansing Cornell
and mother, Marion Cornell,
my loving Aunt Edith
who always lives in my heart;
and my wonderful and special husband,
Thomas E. Gomberg,
who spurs me on,
and lastly to his wonderful parents,
Samuel and Gladys,
who are like my parents
and whom I love very much

Table of Contents

Introduction

Do you find it difficult or nearly impossible to entice the industrial arts teacher to bring the class to the library? What about the art teacher? Do the home economics and physical education teachers feel that the library media center does not supplement or complement their teaching? Do curriculum teachers feel that English is the only subject whose students really need to use the library for book reports and library skills (with science and history research perhaps a distant second)? If this sounds familiar—if most of the subject instructors of your school are islands unto themselves—read on.

Libraries are no longer passive places tucked away down a hallway, or in a corner of the school. They are alive, active places where learning can and does take place—learning in all areas of the curriculum. The term "library" has been replaced in recent years by "library media center," reflecting both the diversity of materials now available and the library's deserved position at the heart of the school.

This book is intended for the library media specialist and the subject teacher—whatever subject that may be. The purpose of the book is to offer ideas on how the library media center can enrich and enhance learning in all subjects. Some of the ideas give students a practical reason to study a specific subject. The book is not a recipe book, but an idea book. No objectives or lists of materials are to be found here. Any library media specialist or teacher can sit down and write such lists for a specific lesson. What you will find are pithy ideas that will allure all those teachers who never thought of the library as a viable teaching source. When have you ever seen the physical education class make use of a library media center? You will here.

This book suggests contests, games, puzzles (including subject-specific crossword puzzles), fairs, research projects, and other activities for the following areas of the curriculum: art, English, foreign language, guidance, history and geography, home economics, industrial arts, mathematics, microcomputers, music, physical education, and science. I hope that you will find them useful and that they will inspire you to dream up more ideas on your own. Good luck!

I. Art

Art Contest

Display artwork from a number of art classes in the library. The art instructor may select the best works to display. Students may cast a vote for their favorite by secret ballot; the ballot box is located in the library.

Animated Movie

The art class may visit the library media center in order to research cartooning techniques and animation, and may find illustrations and photos to inspire them to create their own animated figures. With the collaboration of the art instructor, the class will produce an animated movie.

Cord Craft

The art class will enjoy this activity. Using ½″ thick cord or wood, paper, pencils, ruler, compass, protractor, hammer, glue or staples, scissors, thread, small nails, masking tape, fabrics, paints, stains, and (if desired) a frame, the class may design art out of string.

Students will first practice constructing triangles, squares, rectangles, circles, arcs, and parallel lines. In addition, they will practice working the basic threading patterns: the horizontal matching, the zig-zag and double zigzag weave, the lattice, and the top-to-bottom pattern.

Art Crossword I

ACROSS

3. This medium is limited to black and shades of gray.
5. Where pottery is placed to fire.
7. The use of light and shade rather than line.
9. Light porous wood used for model building.
11. A cool color.
13. This is used as a binder in oil painting.
15. This allows colors to run freely into one another.
17. Sculptural painting.
18. Japanese art paper.
20. From what school of painting does pointillism come?
23. Most of Amedeo Modigliani's works are _____.
26. What does R mean when applied to paper surfaces?
27. The most famous of the French romantic artists.

DOWN

1. Wax-resist textile process.
2. Carved blocks of wood for printing on paper.
4. Low key colors are colors to which _____ has been added.
6. Tone is color plus _____.
8. Who was the leader of the Fauvism movement?
10. This line is always at eye level.
11. This drawing or underpainting is three-dimensional.
12. The vanishing point is where all receding lines _____.
14. Colors that are applied in one sitting.
16. Where expressionism developed.
18. Who painted "Jacob Blessing the Sons of Joseph"?
19. This movement began in the United States during the late 1950s.
21. These slow down the drying time of acrylic paint.
22. The leading French artist in the Dadaism movement.
24. Who painted "Oarsmen at Chotou"?
25. What is resin?

Art Crossword II

ACROSS

4. Pointillism is painting with small _____.
6. Who painted "The Children's Afternoon at Wargemont"?
8. Another term for silk screening.
10. Encaustic painting involves _____.
12. Beautiful writing and brushwork.
14. This kind of paint is made by mixing powdered pigments with a vegetable oil binder.
15. Watercolor painting can be done in two ways: transparent and _____.
16. Paint applied thickly.
17. Refers to the color itself.
19. Pieter Brueghel the Elder is from which school of painting?
20. Who employed the technique of pointillism?
22. Where surrealism was founded.
24. Japanese art of paper folding.
25. Adobe is earth _____.
27. What color is celadon?
28. A painter from Spain in the late Renaissance.
29. This period of painting replaced rococo; a major movement in the late 1700s and early 1800s.
30. Intensity refers to the _____ of a color.

DOWN

1. A technique in which the painter paints on damp plaster.
2. Who painted "Seated Bather"?
3. In which period did Peter Paul Rubens paint?
5. The Dada movement developed under the influence of _____.
7. Yellow is one of three _____ colors.
9. One of the leading painters of cubism in Spain.
11. Who painted "The Creation of Adam"?
12. The most influential postimpressionist.
13. Claude Monet was the leader of this movement.
15. A creamy white liquid mixture of water, oil, varnish, glue and plaster of Paris.
18. Where did futurism develop?
21. One paints on this.
23. This period of painting developed from the baroque style.
24. Not transparent.
26. This is painted on a wall.

Answers, pp. 115–16.

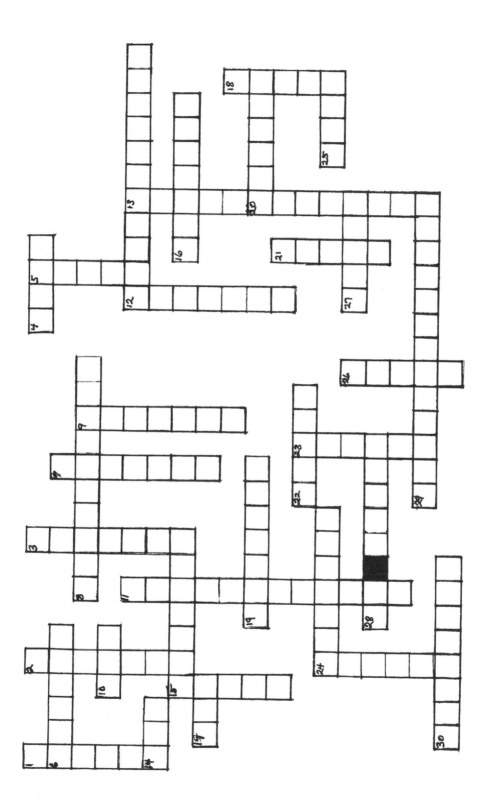

Once students have researched illustrations in the library collection, each student will select and design an object or a picture, and these will be displayed in the library.

Travel Mural

Students of the art class may visit the library media center in order to research the topic of a mural. If, for example, it is to be a mural of the world, each student would research a different country, and would then take notes on what his or her contribution was to be.

Arty Nonsense

The art class may illustrate and paint a picture after visiting the library media center and selecting a limerick or a nonsense verse from which to draw inspiration. These may be exhibited in the library or the hallway, with the limerick or nonsense verse or poem neatly printed or typed under the painting.

Travel Posters

Students from the art class may research in the library media center various countries to serve as the subjects of travel posters. In addition to learning about the character and attractions of each country, they can photocopy photographs to use as models in designing their posters.

Clay Models

The art class may research animals in the library media center, finding photos which may serve as models for clay animal forms. (Photocopies may be taken back to the art room.) These may be displayed in the library media center or in a glass display case located elsewhere in the school.

Paper Sculpture

Students of the art class may visit the library media center in order to locate pictures from which to draw models for their sculpture. These sculptures may be displayed in the library media center. A contest may be held where students can vote for their favorites by secret ballot.

Spring Collage

Students may make a beautiful spring collage out of cut-up old magazines discarded from the library plus their own paintings. The collage may be displayed anywhere in the school. The class would visit the library media center in order to locate photographs of spring flowers, and outdoor scenes.

Advertisements

After studying advertisements from magazines in the library media center, students may make their own advertisements for a product. They will have been instructed as to advertising techniques.

Art Videotape

Videotape a TV program of Bill Alexander or Bob Ross, and invite the art instructor to bring the class into the library media center for a viewing. After the video, have a display of books on art technique to show the class. Many students ask for art technique books.

Art Identification

A sound-slide show may be produced in the library media center reproducing the great masters. Famous works of art by the great painters may be photographed, along with a sound track. We made one of the Impressionists, and it really was quite successful. The art teacher may employ such a slide show to emphasize styles and techniques.

Soft Sculpture

Once again, the library media center may serve as a resource for research in locating illustrations and photographs, this time for soft sculptures, whether for a cartoon character, animal character, or whatever. These may be displayed in the library or elsewhere in the school (we have two glass cases displaying the sculptures in the entrance to our school).

Arty Trends

The library media center is a great place to research recent trends in the art world in reference books and magazines. Locate articles by using the *Readers' Guide*. Students of the art class may locate one or two articles on art trends of today, and then design works representing their own views of art in today's world. These art works may be displayed in the library media center.

Design

Students in the art class may come to the library media center in order to research the elements of design: line, shape, texture, form, color, value and space. They will locate examples of paintings that illustrate how the above elements interact to result in proportion, emphasis, balance, movement and repetition. For example, a student may look for a photograph of a particular painting that emphasizes horizontal lines — serenity and peace. He will then try to emulate this painting in his own work emphasizing horizontal lines. The works may be displayed in the library media center.

II. English

English Bee

This contest may be enjoyable and useful in preparing for a final exam on literature. Devise a list of 75 to 100 questions made up from fiction titles in the media center, and studied by the same English classes. The English or reading instructor and the library media specialist can collaborate on this activity. Students of two English classes are then invited into the library for a "Bee." Alternate questions between the two classes to see who wins. One point could be given for each correct answer.

Classic Quizathon

After the English or reading classes have read a number of classic (or Newbery Award–winning) novels taken from the library media center, invite classes to participate in a Quizathon. Once again, the reading or English teacher and the media specialist may devise a list of questions. Two or more teams may battle over the questions; two or more classes may compete until one team wins the most points. That team should be rewarded with a pizza party.

Addlebrained Alliteration

Students may use the library in order to locate words in a dictionary or thesaurus; or they may find ideas for this activity in the poetry

English Crossword I: Quotations
Who Said...

ACROSS

1. "A well written life is almost as rare as a well-spent one."
3. "As clear as a whistle."
6. "Nobody tells me anything."
10. "Music is the universal language of mankind...."
12. "How often are we forced to charge fortune with partiality towards the unjust."
14. "I'll resk fourty dollars that he can outjump any frog in Calaveras County."

DOWN

2. "The medium is the message."
4. "Amoebas the start were not complex;"
5. "Westminster Abbey, or victory,...."
7. "We shall never understand the natural environment until we see it as a living organism."
8. "O, Susanna!"
9. "Of all the plagues a lover bears,...."
11. "Now is the night one blue dew."
13. "There was an old Man with a beard, who said: It is just as I feared!"

Answers, p. 116.

English Crossword II: Thesaurus

ACROSS

2. (syn) — Gainful.
5. (syn) — Spectral.
10. (syn) — Taint.
11. (syn) — Variable.
12. (syn) — Overshadow.
14. (syn) — Moribund.
17. (syn) — Knowing.
19. (syn) — Laughable.
20. (syn) — Fop.
21. (syn) — Melee.
23. (syn) — Youthful.
26. (syn) — Moot.
29. (syn) — Escapist.
31. (ant) — Backbreaking.

DOWN

1. (syn) — Monomania.
3. (syn) — Overturn.
4. (syn) — Seeming.
6. (syn) — Taciturn.
7. (ant) — Footloose.
8. (syn) — Synthetic.
9. (syn) — Kudos.
13. (ant) — Systematic.
15. (syn) — Lazy.
16. (syn) — Infamous.
18. (ant) — Fervent.
22. (syn) — Flamboyant.
24. (syn) — Sparse.
25. (syn) — Submit.
27. (syn) — Gypsy.
28. (syn) — Plucky.
30. (syn) — Pinnacle.

Answers, p. 116.

section. Each student of the English class prepares a paragraph or more of alliterations, or words that begin with the same sounds. Display these in the media center. The library media specialist can decide which of these paragraphs makes the most sense and tells the best story, and will declare the winner. Use the following two paragraphs for examples:

Jack, a jovial, joyful, jubilant jerk, juggles his judicial job as a judge and jurist of justice and journalist with jumbled jumbo judgment and jabber and jargon just as well as the jack-of-all-trades jingo and jackass and jellyfish.

Jack, the jailer, jailed a jackal of a jaded jailbird, and jabbed the jejune, jazzy jester who jilted Jessica at the jetty as the joker jeopardized Jessica's jewels. Justification justifies the juvenile.

Literary Boxes

Exhibit 20 to 30 boxes with slits cut in the top for viewing the interior. Inside each, mount a synopsis, typed on 2 to 4 index cards, of a fiction book in the library. Exhibit these books around the room. Each student is stationed at one box for one minute or so, until the library media specialist says, "Move on." Then the students have one minute at the next box. After all the students have rotated to all the boxes, they will be divided into two teams. The librarian will read a synopsis and if a student can identify the book, his team gets one point. If he gets it wrong, his team loses a point. The team with the most points wins.

Occupational Addresses

The English class may visit the library in order to locate addresses of associations that they may write letters to, requesting information on occupations. For example, *Occupational Literature: An Annotated Bibliography* by Gertrude Forrester may be used.

Classic Rebus

A rebus is a picture or symbol puzzle representing a word or phrase. Rebuses can be used to denote a title of a book. Prepare several of these, and invite the reading classes who have recently read classics to the library media center. They must guess the correct classic titles. For example:

1. To + mmmmm + (picture of a saw) + 34? (**Tom Sawyer**-Twain)

2. (A picture of an eye) + (a picture of a van) + (a picture of a hoe)? (**Ivanhoe**-Scott)

3. (A picture of a robin) + (a picture of a small boy) + (a picture of a rowing crew or team) + so? (**Robinson Crusoe**-Defoe)

4. (A picture of the sea) + (a picture of a wolf)? (**The Sea Wolf**-London)

5. (A picture of Prince Charles) + (a picture of a paw) + er? (**The Prince and the Pauper**-Twain)

6. 8 + (a picture of cows) + (a picture of an inn)? (**Eight Cousins**-Alcott)

7. Little + (a picture of men)? (**Little Men**-Alcott)

8. The life + (a picture of an advertisement) + ven + tures + of (a picture of a nickel) + as + (a picture of a nickel) + (a picture of a bee)? (**The Life and Adventures of Nicholas Nickleby**-Dickens)

9. Mo + (a picture of a bee) + Dick? (**Moby Dick**-Melville)

10. The + (a picture of a man) + in the + (a picture of an iron) + (a picture of a mask)? (**The Man in the Iron Mask**-Dumas)

11. From the + (a picture of the earth or globe) + to the + (a picture of a moon) + O + the + (a picture of a moon)? (**From the Earth to the Moon and Round the Moon**-Verne)

12. (A picture of a bow) + just? (**Beau Geste**-Wren)

13. (A black square) + (a picture of an arrow)? (**The Black Arrow**-Stevenson)

14. (A green square) + (a picture of huge houses or mansions)? (**Green Mansions**-Hudson)

15. The C + all + of the + (a picture of a forest)? (**The Call of the Wild**-London)

16. (A picture of a kitten mewing) + on the + (a picture of a bow) + N + T)? (**Mutiny on the Bounty**-Nordhoff and Hall)

17. The + (a picture of a red box) + (a picture of a pony)? (**The Red Pony**-Steinbeck)

18. (A picture of an Indian) + new + (a picture of a globe)? (**Brave New World**-Huxley)

19. Weather + ing + (a picture of a mountain)? (**Wuthering Heights**-Brontë)

English Crossword III: *Dracula*

ACROSS

1. Some of the book is made up of entries from this.
6. Mina is placed in a circle of holy _____.
7. The vampire.
9. The fifty-nine-year-old madman.
10. Lucy has a _____ ailment.
12. Dracula doesn't do it.
14. Vampires can turn into a _____.
17. The London solicitor's fiancée.
19. The Russian vessel.
21. Vampires cannot enter a place unless they are _____.
25. The undead can direct the _____.
27. Mina was a homeless _____.
28. Dracula's estate is somewhere in these mountains.
30. What does the vampire become after drinking blood?
33. What is missing in the castle?
34. A ship is sighted here.
35. Lucy does this.
36. A vampire becomes inactive if a wild _____ is placed over it.

DOWN

1. He is sent to Transylvania.
2. What do the vampires become after they die?
3. Lucy's _____ teeth become sharper.
4. He befriends Mina and Lucy.
5. Mina is in a _____.
8. The son of Lord Godalming.
11. The European term meaning the undead.
13. One of Lucy's suitors.
14. They wait at this pier for the ship's arrival.
15. Harker hears about local _____.
16. What frightens Dracula away?
18. He is a doctor, lawyer, a Ph.D., and a D.L.H.
20. A characteristic of the undead: they can't _____.
22. A seaport on the Black Sea.
23. The vampire's power ends at _____.
24. The mysterious woman.
26. This type of book contains suspense.
29. The undead can command them.
31. Harker finds himself in one.
32. It keeps Dracula away.
35. Where did the people on the ship want to throw the box?

Answers, p. 117.

English Crossword IV: *The Pearl*

ACROSS

2. The family is followed by a _____ procession.
4. The town is made up of old natives and _____ settlers.
6. The pearl diver's wife.
7. Kino's family lives in one.
9. Kino hides the pearl under it.
12. Much of the imagery.
14. A group of exploiters.
15. The book begins at this time.
16. The infant son.
17. Kino meets a stranger whom he _____.
19. He refuses to help the baby.
20. Kino's description.
22. Kino mashes the scorpion into a _____.
24. There are many musical themes or _____ that show Kino's feelings.
27. The enemy pursuer.
29. How many men Kino kills.
30. Kino makes it for the baby's shoulder.
32. The story is an _____ legend.
33. What happens to the baby?
35. A short book of this sort is called a _____.
36. They travel at this time.
37. The pearl has many meanings or _____.

DOWN

1. The song of warmth, love and security.
3. Juana and Kino walk side by side; they have been made _____.
5. The pearl diver's brother, Juan _____.
8. They are likened to octopuses.
10. What Kino wants to do with the pearl.
11. The customary way of walking: _____ file.
13. Juan's wife.
16. Kino and Juana hide there.
17. The pearl diver.
18. He thinks of repairs to the church.
21. Kino heads toward this place.
23. Kino lets out a _____.
25. It stings the baby.
26. Time-span of book in days.
28. Kino smashes his hand against it when going for the doctor.
31. The weather as Kino escapes.
34. Some of the animal imagery.

Answers, pp. 117–18.

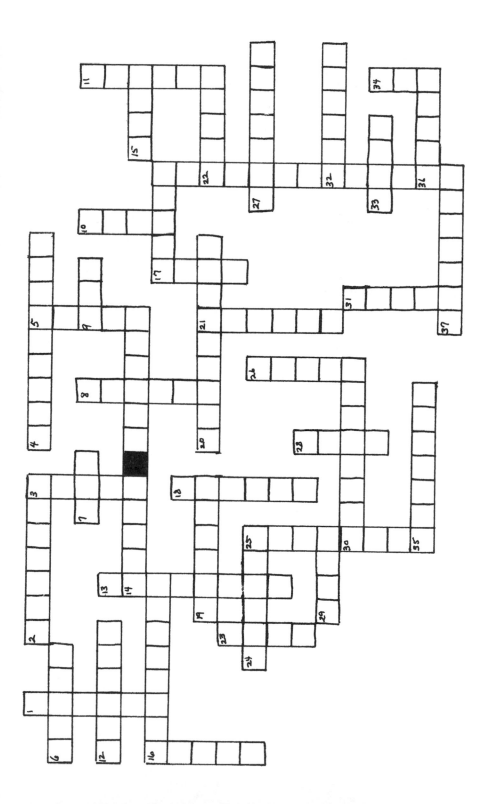

20. (A scarlet square) + (a picture of a letter)? (**The Scarlet Letter**-Hawthorne)

21. (A picture of a dish of pudding) + (a picture of a head) + Wilson? (**Pudd'nhead Wilson**-Twain)

22. The + (a picture of Three Musketeer candy bars)? (**The Three Musketeers**-Dumas)

23. (A picture of daytime) + vid + (a picture of copper pots) + (a picture of a field)? (**David Copperfield**-Dickens)

24. The + (a picture of a bathrobe)? (**The Robe**-Douglas)

25. (A picture of a house) + of the + 7 + (a picture of gables)? (**The House of the Seven Gables**-Hawthorne)

26. The + (a picture of an old man) + and + the + (a picture of the sea)? (**The Old Man and the Sea**-Hemingway)

27. Lost + (a picture of the sunset)? (**Lost Horizon**-Hilton)

28. (A picture of grapes) + of + Wrath? (**Grapes of Wrath**-Steinbeck)

29. The Color + (a purple square)? (**The Color Purple**-Walker)

30. (A picture of a cat) + (a picture of a cradle)? (**Cat's Cradle**-Vonnegut)

Newbery First Lines

This activity could be used as a contest for the library or as a contest between classes or within the same class. Students must identify the title of the Newbery Fiction award–winning book from which the first line was taken. This activity may take place toward the end of the school year when classes have had a chance to read some of the titles.

Reporter

Each student will find four references to magazine articles in the *Readers' Guide*. The topic could be almost anything the student selects. He or she will then locate the articles in the magazines in the library media center. The student will act as a TV news reporter, and prepare a written report on his or her findings. The report can then be presented to the class.

General Reference Talk

Upon visiting the library media center, the English class will be shown numerous examples of reference books: bibliographies, indexes and abstracts, special subject encyclopedias, special subject dictionaries, books on quotations, almanacs and special subject almanacs, guides and handbooks and manuals, directories, biographical and geographical sources, government documents, yearbooks and annuals, and statistical reference sources. Later, the class can be given an assignment from their teacher, and students will then have an opportunity to utilize the reference collection. This reference talk is very successful at our school, and students really get a lot out of it.

Talk Show

This activity can be used in almost any of the subject areas of the curriculum. In the English class, for example, each person would come to the library media center to research a famous person, such as Marie Curie, Louis Pasteur, David Livingstone, various sports figures, etc. After the students have researched reference sources in the library and checked out biographies on their subjects, each student assumes the character of his subject to appear as a guest on a "talk show." The teacher or library media specialist interviews the guests to find out about their lives. A panel of perhaps five guests could be interviewed at one time.

English "Jeopardy"

This activity is borrowed from the popular TV show, and may inspire participation from all the subjects in the curriculum. The library media specialist may work with the teachers who wish to join in on this active and fun game. Specific topics from the English and reading curriculum may be selected by the teacher and library media specialist. For example, anything that has been studied in the classroom may be used as a broad general category such as quotations, biographical names, fiction books in all categories, plays, poetry, authors, reference tools, folklore, etc.

English Crossword V: *The Hobbit*

ACROSS

2. What do the trolls turn into at dawn?
4. Bilbo _____.
6. The treasure.
7. Took blood.
8. Where does Gandalf want to go?
9. Who is at the door on the next day?
11. What does he do with Gandalf?
13. "A small slimy creature."
14. They go on their journey by this mode of transportation.
15. Bilbo plans to send the dwarves downstream by way of _____.
16. Is everything in an upheaval at the end of the book?
18. All the creatures seek or reject it.
22. Thorin wishes to be _____ with Bilbo.
26. Bilbo returns home to the _____.
27. Bilbo and the mysterious creature play a game of _____.
28. What item does Gandalf reveal for the journey?
29. The setting of the novel.
34. "Relations of ours."
35. Bombur falls into a _____.
36. The greatest treasure.

DOWN

1. Bilbo's favorite pleasure.
3. The only dwarf not taken.
4. Where Bilbo lives.
5. What is Gandalf?
9. What is Smaug?
10. Who falls into the water?
12. What ties Bilbo down?
17. Thorin _____.
19. Bilbo is always thought of as _____.
20. Their friend.
21. The battle of the _____.
23. What happens to Smaug?
24. Who tells of Smaug's weak spot?
25. What kind of ring Bilbo puts into his pocket.
30. The destination of the barrels.
31. Gandalf kills the great _____.
32. How many come all together?
33. Smaug reveals a _____ not covered.

Answers, p. 118.

English Crossword VI: *Moby Dick*

ACROSS

1. The narrator of the story.
3. Moby Dick has a white _____.
5. A school of whales.
6. He is from the Town-Ho and persecuted.
9. What happens to Moby Dick?
11. The minister.
13. Ahab constantly reads these.
14. The captain is confined to his cabin because he is _____.
15. The third harpooner who is descended from Africa.
17. The Rachel's missing crew includes the captain's _____.
19. The book does not always deal with black and white; it deals in _____.
21. A storm forces the narrator to stay at this chapel.
23. The black cabin boy.
25. Sometimes Melville's style is like _____ poetry.
26. The ship's first mate.

DOWN

2. The narrator is from _____.
3. The third mate.
4. Some of the style.
5. The crazy prophet on the *Jeroboam*.
7. The novel deals with good and _____.
8. Moby Dick has a deformed _____.
10. The narrator's friend who is a harpooner.
11. The ship's cook.
12. The mysterious dark figures.
16. The captain of the ship.
18. Ishmael and Queequeg get a whaling ship there.
20. The ocean where Moby Dick is found.
22. Captain of the *Jeroboam*.
24. What happens to the three mast tips?

Answers, pp. 118–19.

English Crossword VII: *Kidnapped*

ACROSS

   3. The sixteen-year-old boy.
   5. A Highland money changer.
   7. Lord of the house.
   9. Colin of Glenure is the "Red _____."
10. Alan is loyal to _____.
11. Alan carries them.
12. David's father is the _____ son.
16. He brings a message to Mrs. Stewart.
20. Mr. Campbell is its minister.
21. What is "Cluny's cage"?
23. First mate aboard the *Covenant*.
25. A James of the Glens' agent.
27. Alan wants to be ruled by a _____.
29. They come to a place, _____ and-be-thankful.
31. Thought of as a witch.
32. The main island.

DOWN

   1. A major rebel.
   2. Mr. Stewart.
   4. Much of the dialogue in this book is written in regional _____.
   6. His schoolmaster father.
   8. A cabin-boy on the *Covenant*.
13. Robin Oig is one of the sons.
14. They lived in the Heugh of _____ for five days.
15. A wandering catechist.
17. The stranger wants to go to _____ Loch.
18. An exiled captain of Alan's clan.
19. A Queensferry lawyer.
22. Pseudonym for Alan Breck Stewart.
24. David is warned to avoid the _____.
26. Color of the buttons.
28. David wonders if his father and uncle were _____.
30. Some of the scenery.

Answers, p. 119.

Students may be given the topics, and most of the questions that would be asked during the actual game. They would come to the library media center with their class prior to the game in order to research the answers.

This game could be a battle between a number of classes, or a battle among members of the same English class. The librarian could prepare on the bulletin board or an overhead transparency the various categories that each student may choose from, and could read the questions to each player. The student would receive 5 points for each correct answer, and 5 points could be deducted from the score for each incorrect answer. At the end of one session, new students could participate in the game, allowing the winner to compete against another two students.

Tell Me a Story

Students will come to the library media center to select a book of short stories (perhaps a collection of stories about a specific theme — western, science fiction, Irish stories, etc. — or a collection of stories by a particular writer, such as Edgar Allan Poe, Isaac Asimov, or O. Henry). Upon reading the selection, the student will select his favorite story from this collection to tell the class.

Figures of Speech

The English class may visit the library media center in order to locate examples of figures of speech such as similes and metaphors in the library resources. Students may find everyday uses of these in advertisements in the magazines and newspapers, and in the poetry section. Examples of other figures of speech, such as personification, metonymy and synecdoche, may also be found.

Free Materials Box

Using *Exceptional Free Library Resource Materials* by Carol Smallwood (Libraries Unlimited, 1984) and other resources, send away for free materials that would be of supplemental use in the curriculum. Place a variety of materials in a special box and inform teachers and students of the box. Materials from many sources and of numerous topics are available.

Parts of Speech

The English class may examine newspapers, magazines and books to find examples of nouns, verbs, adjectives and adverbs. Students may, for example, choose the comics in the newspaper to find examples.

III. Foreign Language

Expressions

Students from the foreign language class may visit the library media center in order to locate foreign language expressions in newspapers and magazines and books. For instance, the French class may be advised to watch for some of the following expressions: affaire d'amour (love affair); au revoir (till we meet again); bête noir (black beast; an object of abhorrence); bonjour (good day; good morning); bon voyage (good voyage to you); bon soir (good evening); cherchez la femme (seek the woman); en rapport (in sympathetic relation); entre nous (between ourselves; confidentially); fait accompli (an accomplished fact); laissez-nous faire (let us be; let us alone); mal de mer (sea sickness); n'est-ce pas (is it not so?); nom de plume (literally, a pen name; a pseudonym); pâté de foie gras (a pie of fat goose livers); raison d'être (reason for being; an excuse for existing); s'il vous plaît (if you please); respondez s'il vous plaît (RSVP, reply if you please); esprit de corps (common devotion of the members of an organization).

Translation

The foreign language class may come to the library media center to translate an article from a foreign language magazine; also they may take a newspaper article, and translate it into French or Spanish.

Foreign Directions

Upon visiting the library media center, the foreign language class will be given written instructions in Spanish or French such as: "Find a fiction book by A. Dumas"; "Find the depth of the deepest part of the Pacific Ocean"; "Find a magazine article in the *Readers' Guide* about space travel"; etc. Each student must complete his or her assignment successfully. Each student may be given two instructions: one being to locate a specific book, and one being to locate a specific article or answer in a reference book. Each student would be given a 50 or 100 if he or she locates the book, and 100 for the effort of finding the correct answers.

Spelling Bee

The foreign language class may utilize the foreign language reference dictionaries in the library media center. Given a list of words, they may look up their definitions in preparation for a spelling bee.

Culture Week

Students in the French and Spanish classes may visit the library media center in order to research cultural understanding of the Spanish- and French-speaking countries; Spain and France into the 1980s; religion and tradition; daily life; sports; entertainment and cultural pastimes; education; history and politics; travel and tourism.

French Café

The foreign language class can visit the library in order to research French desserts. They will then whip up a few of their choices at home or in conjunction with the home economics class, and bring these to the French café.

Foreign Language Crossword I

ACROSS

1. Swedish — Authority.
4. Polish — Ticket.
6. Yiddish — Starch.
8. Polish — Way.
11. Esperanto — Mistake.
12. Spanish — Yellow.
13. Indonesian — Birthday.
16. Turkish — Dance.
17. Hebrew — Camel.
19. Dutch — Tedious.
20. Indonesian — Skis.
21. Russian — Hail.
22. German — Garlic.
26. Japanese — King.
29. Arabic — Subway.
30. Polish — April.
31. Finnish — Teacher.

DOWN

1. Swahili — Cocoa.
2. Arabic — Point.
3. Finnish — Drown.
4. French — Cheap.
5. Polish — Tax.
7. Japanese — Three.
9. Serbo-Croat — Slowly.
10. Esperanto — Tie.
14. Hungarian — Play.
15. Yiddish — Industy.
18. Greek — Dictionary.
23. Swahili — Give.
24. Rumanian — Pin.
25. French — Chemistry.
27. Finnish — Meat.
28. French — Life.

Answers, pp. 119–20.

Foreign Language Crossword II: French

ACROSS

3. To mend.
6. Breeding cage.
8. Walnut.
9. Filling with mud.
10. Watchtower.
11. Play.
14. Incense.
15. Queen.
18. A small pushcart.
19. To dare.
21. A study.
22. To skin.
23. Interview.
25. Frowning.
30. Crackle.
32. Remède means _____.
33. Neighbouring.
35. What is a mécanicien?

DOWN

1. Stumbling.
2. To frizz the hair.
4. Obviously.
5. Expatriate.
7. Report.
12. Simpleton.
13. Father.
16. Supreme.
17. Little.
20. Here.
24. To rejoin.
25. To get thin again.
26. Frippery.
27. Born.
28. Rope.
29. Woman.
31. Convincing.
34. Foot.

Answers, p. 120.

Spanish Fiesta

Once again, the Spanish language class will come to the library media center in order to explore costumes to wear, party foods to make, decorations to make, and games to play for a Spanish fiesta.

Tête-à-Tête

Students may locate magazine or newspaper articles in the library media center in order to translate bits and pieces of these articles for a French conversation. Students can engage in pairs in spontaneous, interactive French conversation on everyday topics.

Foreign Fiction

The library media center holds numerous fiction titles in both French and Spanish on various levels of difficulty for students to borrow. A few of these are classic titles, and many others are more simplified versions of classic stories, or other such stories.

Radio News Broadcast

Students of the foreign language class may research numerous news stories in the library media center in order to write their own newscast. Magazines and newspapers may serve as the sources of information.

Spanish-French Bingo

Students will visit the library to create and design bingo cards by locating appropriate words and phrases in Spanish and French dictionaries. *Cassell's French-English, English-French Dictionary* (Macmillan, 1962) and the *New Revised Velazquez Spanish and English Dictionary* (New Century, 1985) are a couple of excellent sources.

Pen Pals

Students may utilize the library media center in order to write letters to pen pals with the aid of a foreign language dictionary.

French Video

Videotape a TV French lesson, or purchase French and Spanish movies. Make these available to the foreign language classes.

Language Lab

Students may frequent the library media center in order to listen to foreign language tapes, cassettes or records over earphones. They may be required to listen to tapes on a weekly basis.

Foreign Language Rebus

This may be a challenge for the foreign language class. Students may compose a rebus, which is a series of letters and pictures that represent a word or group of words. Common everyday objects as well as people, events, almost anything may be represented. The idea of the activity is to locate illustrations in books or magazines. Photographs from reference books may be photocopied. The class must guess what the clues of the puzzle are, and put them together. They, of course, must speak in Spanish or French. For example: a picture of a man = l'homme in French; a picture of a book and a map = géographie in French.

IV. Guidance

Career Clusters

Each class of the curriculum could do this activity. The math class may visit the library media center in order to research careers related to mathematics. For instance, technical analyst and engineer; accountant; banker; actuary; statistician; insurance salesman; economist; business statistician; bookkeeper; surveyor; etc. Other careers less directly related to math also have mathematical aspects and can be included, such as carpentry. Students will make a giant poster out of oak tag and construction paper, scissors, glue and magic markers and stencils. Each student would locate and list as many careers as possible. On the large poster, the class places a circle or square with "mathematics" printed inside of it. Then students make smaller boxes or circles with the various careers printed inside, emanating from the central larger box or circle. This can be displayed in the library media center or outside the math room.

Career Game

Any class may visit the library media center in order to research many kinds of careers. Each student will be given one occupation printed on a card. He or she will research this occupation thoroughly. The class will come back to the media center at a later date, and will be divided into two teams. They will have prepared questions to ask the opposite team in order for that team to guess the correct occupation. Twenty points are given to that team if they guess the career in five questions or fewer. Five points are given if the team guesses the career in six to ten questions, and one point is given if they answer in eleven to twenty questions. The team with the most points wins. Each student will have prepared at least twenty questions. The careers may be appropriate to the class subject.

Body Language Bazaar

The library media specialist and the guidance department may collaborate on this activity to increase awareness of non-verbal communication and what it means, such as posture, gestures, eye contact, and body spaces.

The library media specialist may locate a book on body language, and reproduce various examples. After showing these to the class, each student will be asked to react to a command by body language. For example, the library media specialist or guidance counselor might ask a student to show the class how he looks when he is nervous.

Bibliotherapy

The guidance department, the social worker and the psychologist can work with the library media specialist in suggesting appropriate non-fiction titles relating to divorce; child abuse; single-parent families orphans; brother and sister relationships; friendships; poverty; physical handicaps; pregnancy; minorities; hospitals and disease; mental handicaps; suicide; juvenile delinquency; family situations; death; drug problems; the elderly; emotional problems; adolescence. Students may be sent to the library media center in order to review titles on various problems. Likewise, the library media specialist can make up bibliographies for the guidance, social work and psychology departments so that they may suggest these to students.

Summer Jobs

The library media center may be a center for locating summer employment in *Summer Opportunities for Kids & Teenagers,* a Peterson

Guidance Crossword I

ACROSS

3. This can be a dangerous career; driving from track to track.
4. Stuffs dead animals.
6. He maps a construction project.
8. Your personality makes customers want to come back; you serve them.
9. Intrigued by money, and interested in people.
10. Studies the races of man, the similarities and differences among peoples.
13. A child's doctor.
14. A life and death profession; giving medication and care.
15. A foot doctor.
18. This person must have drive to win in the world of bread.
19. He serves people's social and spiritual needs.

DOWN

1. Works with the leaders of tomorrow.
2. He brings books and people together.
5. This career has success and failure every week; directs people in plays.
7. This person interviews people for stories.
11. He helps the nurse to care for patients.
12. Handles calls with efficiency.
16. Designs buildings.
17. This person molds and forms, and often must work on commission.

Answers, p. 120.

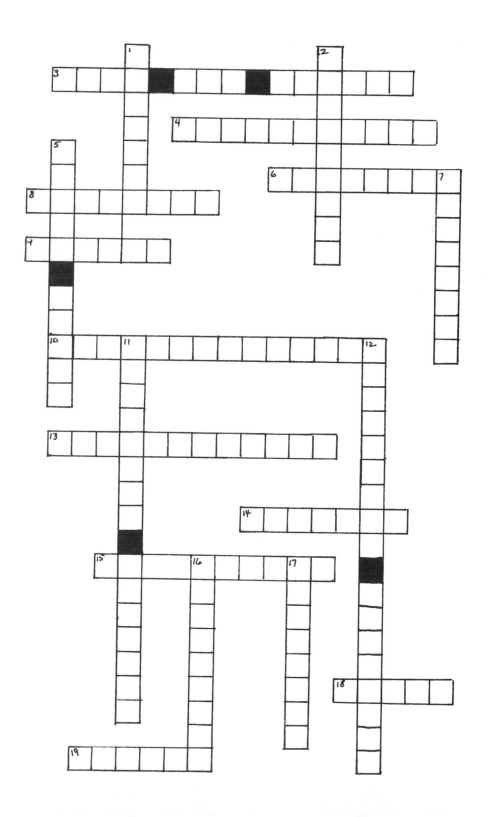

Guidance Crossword II

ACROSS

2. To relate to people, good _____ skills are important.
8. This is always a good policy.
11. One stressful emotion.
12. How to help your conversational ability.
14. Teens are separating more from the _____, and trying to find a group.
15. Everyone can _____ in something.
18. This person likes fewer friends, and enjoys being alone.
19. Good students use their _____ wisely.
23. These can kill you.
24. Your earliest _____ are learned from your parents.
25. Usually boys have fewer restrictions about the time they must be home, or _____.
26. Another stressful emotion.
28. To be a good student, work quietly in the same _____.
29. A person who lets life go by without getting much involved.

DOWN

1. One should strive to have a _____ attitude.
3. These can change in the course of a day.
4. An excellent skill to have, and one that makes for good friends, is to be a good _____.
5. One doesn't always have to do this with parents or friends.
6. How to help your conversational ability.
7. Everyone must make his own _____.
9. Don't be afraid to say _____ if you feel uncomfortable.
10. One should always be thoughtful and _____ in dealing with others.
13. A person who loves a lot of contact with many people.
16. A person who does a lot of things and keeps busy.
17. One can tell a lot about the other person's moods by his _____.
20. These are taught to us as youngsters.
21. Usually, boys are more action-minded and _____ than girls.
22. To overcome shyness, stop thinking of _____.
27. One should not judge others or be prejudiced because of _____.

Answers, p. 121.

Guide. Teens can find many opportunities in the arts, camp jobs, traditional camping, travel, sports, wilderness trips, science and computer fun, and academic opportunities both here and abroad. The media center may serve as a clearinghouse for information.

Animal Careers

Students who enjoy working with animals can find *Careers Working with Animals* by Guy Hodge (The Humane Society of the United States) a valuable resource in the library. Students can read about various animal career profiles, education required, training and experience. Many students at this level love animals.

Guidance Gaming

In conjunction with the guidance and psychology departments, the library media specialist can devise and produce a game in which the goal is assimilation of information. Any topics relating to careers, psychology and guidance can be utilized. A number of board games or simple games between two teams can be devised and utilized in the library media center.

Reserve Career Shelf

The library media center houses several career reference sources plus booklets and pamphlets. Students very often come to the media center in order to peruse these references, and to photocopy information that they are interested in.

Military Career Day

Information pamphlets, general circulation books and reference books plus directories of addresses may provide lots of information on military careers. Portions of *The Military Career Guide* from the United States Military Entrance Processing Command can be photocopied for students to take, and people from the military may be invited to spend a short time at the school speaking on the Navy, Army, and Marines.

Job Descriptions

Students can utilize materials in the media center in order to write job descriptions for specific careers. Careers require different attitudes, abilities and interests. These job descriptions are posted in the library media center or throughout the school. Students may "advertise" these over the school radio. Other students interested will fill out application forms. They will then be called for a "job interview" by an "employment bureau" which screens the applicants.

Rap Sessions

The library media center can sponsor informal "rap sessions" on specific topics, such as friends, self-confidence, positive thinking, values, feelings, appearance, social skills, etc. The guidance, social work or psychology department can lead these rap sessions. The library media center provides a convenient place to meet as well as numerous books to share on these topics.

Career Fair

Invite career specialists from all walks of life to come to the school library media center to speak to students at the Career Fair. Pamphlets could be reproduced for give-outs, plus photocopied materials from the library media center can be made available. Addresses of associations for additional information may also be made available.

Community Field Trips

The library media specialist can make arrangements for field trips to various job sites in the community. If at all possible, photographs, videos, and tape recordings could be utilized to store in the media center for future use. Classes not going on the field trips can then benefit from the experiences.

Guidance Video

Purchase commercial videos on social skills, values, appearance, self-confidence and friendship. Advertise to the guidance, social work and psychology departments the availability of these videos.

Bibliotherapy Session

Give book talks on fiction titles depicting problems such as adolescence, drugs, step-families, physical handicaps, mental handicaps, emotional handicaps, juvenile delinquency, family problems, disease, etc.

V. History and Geography

Photo Probe

Select and photocopy photographs taken from history reference books, and give one to each student of the social studies class. Students must study the photos, do some library research, and decide from what periods of history the photos come. Students must identify the when, where, who and what of the photos. Each student is assigned the task of discovering exactly what is happening in his or her picture, and writing a brief report for the class.

United Nations Conference

This activity may be more suited for the upper tract and gifted students. Each student would represent one nation, for example, Libya, the Soviet Union, etc. The United States may be represented by more than one student. Each student would research and write a one to two page paper on each country, primarily stating the political position held by that country. For example, Libya has been accused of terrorism by the United States, and of course denies it. Explain Libya's position and viewpoint, and how it fits into the world. Also, students may include information about each country such as population, geography, type of government, economy, finance, transport, etc. However, the majority of the paper would be stating the country's political position in the world. How does that country contribute to or take away from the peace of the world? The social studies or history class may research various reference books and magazines in the library, then hold the "conference" in the library or the classroom.

American History Crossword

ACROSS

3. President of the United States 1801–09.
6. From what country did the United States purchase Alaska?
8. What was discovered in California in 1848?
11. The 1854 Kansas-_____ act.
13. This organization began in 1946 for world peace.
15. The American Federation of _____ formed in 1886.
18. This crash in 1929 brought financial ruin to many.
19. What Benjamin Franklin flew in a storm to prove that lightning is electricity.
20. In the 1800s, businesses formed them; they are illegal today.
21. The war that began in the United States in 1861.
22. Who was United States president 1829–37?

DOWN

1. A United States purchase in 1803.
2. An 1823 doctrine.
4. This canal was opened in 1825.
5. United States president 1860–65.
7. This canal was completed in 1914.
9. United States president 1933–45.
10. He wrote "The Star-Spangled Banner."
12. The first commercial steam train.
14. The war of 1898.
16. Woodrow Wilson's political party.
17. Who mass-produced the Model T car?
18. Robert Fulton's invention.

Answers, p. 121.

Geography Crossword

ACROSS

1. What is Phet Buri?
3. What is Jacquinot Bay?
4. Saint Laurent is a town in _____.
5. How is Stonehenge arranged?
6. What is Cluny?
7. Where is Luca?
11. What is Cairn Hill?
12. How many miles long is the Kashaar River?
14. An island of Indonesia.
16. Where is the Maringa?
18. A seaport on the island of We off Indonesia.
23. What is the Hado?
24. Where is Nizib?
26. Augusta is a county there.
29. This river is 365 miles long in Quebec, and flows into the Hudson Bay.
30. What is Saint Clairsville?
31. Where is Nafada?

DOWN

1. What is Kuwait?
2. These mountains are in Iran, along the Iran-Iraq border.
4. An ancient town on the Danube.
6. Where is Cnidus?
8. The Bald Mountains are part of what mountain chain?
9. What kind of commune is Angleur?
10. Karenni is a district in _____.
13. Where is the river Pharpar?
15. What is Manhattan?
16. Cape Saint Eli is off of what coast?
17. Misr is the modern name for _____.
19. Where is Sangli?
20. Northfleet is an _____ district in England.
21. Teller is a county in _____.
22. One of the nine states of Malaya.
25. What shape is Laguna?
27. What color is the Dighton Rock?
28. What is the Chobe?

Answers, pp. 121–22.

Indiana Indians

Each member of the geography or history class will locate and name a place in the state of Indiana that sounds like an Indian tribe. The student who lists the most correct answers wins. Students will utilize reference materials in the library in order to accomplish this goal.

1. Crow
2. Cheyenne
3. Sioux
4. Mohawk
5. Apache
6. Pueblo
7. Ute Peak
8. Massachusetts
9. Delaware
10. Narraganset
11. Mohave Desert
12. Erie
13. Ottawa
14. Illinois
15. Oneida
16. Comanche
17. Missouri
18. Navajo
19. Iowa
20. Chickasaw
21. Cherokee
22. Miami
23. Omaha
24. Bannock
25. Choctaw

Historical Interview

Students may locate information in the school library media center through reference books, the general collection, the vertical file, etc., about a person living during and associated with the Revolutionary War. Some examples are George Washington; Thomas Jefferson; John Stark; Lord Charles Cornwallis; John Adams; Samuel Adams; King George III of England; Marquis de Lafayette; Nathanael Greene; Tadeusz Kościuszko; Josiah Quincy, Jr.; Banastre Tarleton; Anthony Wayne.

Select some personal information about this person. Write an "interview" with this person as it might appear in a newspaper. Students may spend several days in the library researching. Each may display his or her interview in the library after having read it out loud to the class.

You Were There

The class researches historical figures of the period they are study-ing in history. For example, if studying the Revolutionary War, each member of the class will research one famous person from that era and write a one-page, first-person report (that is, the student will assume his subject's identity). The report should stress the person's accomplish-ments, and what he or she did that makes him or her remembered. Students may read their reports onto tape after they are approved by the teacher, and the tape recordings may be played at a later date. Other students must identify who the voices are, that is, what famous person each voice portrays.

Geography Bee

Students in one geography class may compete with students in another geography class, or all the geography classes in the school may compete against one another in this contest. A list of geographical ques-tions may be given to the students so that they may research the answers in the library media center.

I Was There

The history class may participate in this activity. They must imag-ine that they fought on the Patriot side in one of the famous battles of the American Revolution. They must write an account of what hap-pened. In order to do this, they must research the theme in the li-brary.

Colonial Cartoon

The history class may enjoy this activity. Draw a cartoon il-lustrating the feeling of the colonists about one of the following: the Proclamation of 1763; the Stamp Act; or the Intolerable Acts. Again, students must do research in the school media center.

Colonial Project

The history class will research colonial times topics in the library in order to make a diorama, illustration, or exhibit, and to write a two-page report. Some examples of topics may be: quilting; doll-making (corn-husk or apple, etc.); colonial scrapbooks; collage; broom-making; candle-making; tin can lanterns; pottery; herb drying; bread-making; colonial cookbooks; how-to books; stenciling; quilling; embroidery; food preserving; flower drying; food preparation such as breads, cookies, cornbread, taffy, Indian pudding, stew, candy; weaving; wool carding and spinning. Projects will be exhibited in the library upon completion.

Colonial Fruits and Vegetables

The history class may research in the library media center what fruits and vegetables were here in North America when Jamestown (1607) was established. Students may include the entire continent of North America as the subject of their research.

Diorama: United States History

The history class may be divided into groups of three. Each group of students will make a diorama (a three-dimensional reproduction of an event), do research and present an oral report to the class on a specific topic. The topic may be any event leading to the Civil War, any event occurring during the Civil War, or any event through Lincoln's assassination related to the Civil War. Suggested topics: the invention of the cotton gin; the use of the cotton gin; States' rights debate (Hayne vs. Webster) of 1830. Scenes may be Uncle Tom's cabin; "Bleeding Kansas"; Lincoln-Douglas debate; any battle from the Civil War; Dred Scott decision; Harper's Ferry; firing on Ft. Sumter; Emancipation Proclamation; *Monitor* vs. *Merrimac*; Appomattox Court House; Lincoln's assassination. Members of the group will do independent research and write a two-page report on their topic.

Flags

The geography class will visit the library to research world flags. Once they have had an opportunity to study the flags, a contest may be arranged in the form of a spelling bee. The geography teacher or the library media specialist will photocopy or cut up an old book of flags, and make up flash cards. Each student will correctly identify the flag shown; if that student does not, he or she is eliminated from competition. The last student left in the competition is the winner.

Where in the World

A map is used for this activity, either a pull-down hanging map, or a giant map on the bulletin board. The class is divided into two teams. The class is given a list of about 50 cities around the world. They must initially check in the library media center the location of each city by atlases and the *Webster's Geographical Dictionary*. Each student gets a piece of paper with one city listed on it. Alternating between the two teams, each student must place a finger on the location of the city within seven seconds. If the student is correct, that team receives a point. If not, they lose a point. The geography teacher may judge the correct answers. The team with the most correct answers wins.

History Book

Students may visit the library media center a number of times to research an era of history, so that they may compile a three-chapter "book." These books may be exhibited in the library media center.

Hot Debate

Students of the social studies or history class may go to the school library media center to explore and research topics for debating. Books and pamphlets in the Greenhaven Press "Opposing Viewpoints" series include many hot topics of today for debates. AIDS, abortion, drug testing, nuclear power, gun control, genetic engineering, the United States role in the Middle East, and drugs in sports are only a handful of possible topics found in the references in the library media center.

VI. Home Economics

Fashion Show

With the help of the home economics teacher, prepare a slide show or a video showing the elements of clothing design — silhouette, color, line, proportion, balance and texture — and showing students how to select clothing.

The video or slide show may show how to identify body shape — the rectangle, the inverted triangle, the triangle, the hourglass — and explain how to match clothing to the shape. In addition, how to use line and color to bring out the best in each figure could be explained.

Once students have viewed the "Fashion Show" video, have a real fashion show in the library. Each student in the home economics class will receive one point for wearing an outfit with the correct silhouette for her body shape; one point for the correct use of lines to conceal weight, emphasize height or control image; and one point for the proper use of color to emphasize or minimize her size. The home economics teacher and the library media specialist may collaborate as the fashion judges.

Fabric Fair

The home economics class may come to the library for this activity. The library media specialist, with the cooperation of the home economics teacher, collects swatches of various types of material: corduroy, terry cloth, different types of silk, single and double knits, interlock knits, flannel, velveteen or velvet, worsted gabardine, linen, wool and woolen tweed, viscose satin, taffeta, cotton, etc. A magnifying glass may be used to examine fibers closely.

Students will examine the various types of fabrics. They may research information about each fabric by using reference books. Students may be given an outline sheet by their teacher indicating what they should look for, for example:

—the difference between a pile weave and a napped fabric.
—how a weave and a knit differ.
—differences between warp and weft knits, and between single and double knits.
—differences between natural and cultivated silk.
—the look and feel of linen.
—how corduroy differs from flannel and velveteen.

Kitchen Korner

In cooperation with the home economics instructor, prepare a slide show or video on the proper equipment and choices of equipment used in the kitchen. Indicate the advantages and disadvantages of aluminum, anodized aluminum, copper, stainless steel, cast iron, ceramic, enamelware and glass. Quality construction may be emphasized in bakeware, cooking pans and other utensils. Also, indicate how to know the best cutlery, how to keep the blades sharp, and techniques for the various types of knives such as slicing knives, paring knives, chef's knives, carving knives, etc.

Happy Housework

With the assistance of the home economics teacher and reference materials such as *Speed Cleaning* by Jeff Campbell and The Clean Team (Dell 1985), design a slide show on the easiest, fastest and most efficient way of cleaning house. Indicate why housecleaning often seems so tough, and that sometimes we make more work through our methods than we save. Show slides of the correct tools to use; the most effective methods of housecleaning developed by the professionals; and the type of cleansers that we need to use (emphasizing that only a few are really needed).

Home Economics
Crossword I: Cooking

ACROSS

2. A French main dish of bacon, cream and eggs.
5. This national dish of Spain is cooked in a shallow skillet.
6. A thin wood or metal stick used for meat and vegetables for broiling and grilling.
8. To push food through a sieve to make a thick pulp.
9. French pancakes.
11. An ingredient that causes dough to rise.
12. What is dijon?
14. Greek spinach pie.
16. A powdered, clear protein used to thicken.
17. These are used in many Greek recipes for wrapping fillings.
20. A kind of green onion.
21. This sauce was originally made in Worcester, England, and is delicious with steak.

DOWN

1. These are small, dried, seedless grapes very much like raisins.
3. What the Chinese eat with.
4. A root used to flavor Chinese food.
7. Lebanese appetizers.
10. To cook slowly in a covered pot with liquid.
12. To soak food in liquid to tenderize and add flavor.
13. A very hot red pepper.
15. A small wire tool for beating by hand.
18. A category of Japanese cooking comprised of hearty one-pot meals cooked at the table.
19. A fine white starch made from corn.
20. Indian pastries.

Answers, p. 122.

Home Economics
Crossword II: Sewing

ACROSS

3. When you can't thread your needle, you use this.
4. Pin heads are flat, "T," or _____.
5. A T-square is used for finding _____.
9. A decorative hem finish used often for linens or handkerchiefs.
12. These are folds in the fabric that give controlled fullness.
13. Cotton is a _____ fiber.
15. To sew loosely for easy removal.
19. This is used to mark hems.
20. This is used for threading cord or elastic through a casing.
21. A decorative stitched fold of material.
22. The type of sewing needle used most often.

DOWN

1. This is handy when re-drawing construction lines on patterns.
2. This is used to reinforce the fabric.
6. Two flat and small pressing surfaces on which seams and details can be pressed on sleeves, pant legs, etc.
7. A safe place to store pins.
8. On the sewing machine, the all-purpose foot is also called the _____.
10. This transfers constructed markings on both sides of the fabric.
11. This is a strip of material that encases a garment edge or hem.
14. Fabric cut at a diagonal at a 45-degree angle.
16. Zippers are conventional, invisible, and _____.
17. These are spool-like thread holders.
18. Gathered stitches.

Answers, p. 122.

Make-Up Mart

The home economics teacher and the library media specialist may ask a local beauty expert to visit the school library for a small fee. This may also be considered an endorsement to the beauty shop.

Students may be used as models. The beauty specialist may show correct make-up techniques, and how to put one's best face forward. A number of the girls may serve as examples, and if there is time, each member of the class should be included.

Sewing Scraps

The library media specialist will collect and reproduce photographs and illustrations of sewing equipment, specific types of stitching, pattern symbols, parts of a sewing machine, etc. The home economics teacher may contribute actual samples of these. In the library, the class will be divided into three teams. The library media specialist and home economics teacher will show the reproduced photos, illustrations, and samples to the class, and each student must identify each item correctly. Alternating students, the team with the most points will win. This contest may be used toward the end of the year or end of the sewing segment, as a review for the final exam.

Mexican Banquet

After researching Mexican cooking in the library, students from the home economics class will prepare several dishes. Samplings of the food may be kept at booths or stations in the library media center or elsewhere. Students may sample the various foods. Good choices are fried tortillas with cheese; beef tostadas con carne; tacos; Mexican rice; guacamole; frijoles refritos (refried beans); chicken enchiladas; Mexican hot chocolate; nachos. A student committee may decorate the library media center for the event.

Babysitting Bash

Students in the home economics class will visit the library media center to research the topic of babysitting. Students should be given an outline to guide their research: the essential rules for babysitting; finding a job; establishing rates; transportation; safety precautions; children of all ages; infants; feeding baby; changing baby; nap time; play time; etc. Students may fill in answers to questions on their outlines.

Consumer Shopping

Students may come to the library media center in order to study consumer shopping. Each student will have an item to buy, and must find the best quality and lowest price by checking the newspapers and magazines, particularly the *Consumer Reports* and *Buying Guide.*

Nutrition

The home economics class can visit the library media center to research good nutrition. *Everything you always wanted to know about nutrition* by David Reuben, M.D. (Avon 1978) is only one of several good sources. Students can list the vitamins, minerals, elements, fat, carbohydrate and protein content found in various foods by checking references. They could design sample healthful meals for breakfast, lunch and dinner.

Home Health Care

Students may research in the library media center ways of caring for a sick person, preparing a sickroom, emotional needs of a patient and handling communicable diseases. Each student may be given a health emergency or illness in order to research the proper care and handling of that particular problem: for instance, burns, insect bites, measles, poison ivy, flu, food poisoning, etc.

Household Hints

Students in the home economics class may research in the library media center ways of solving various household problems. *Mary Ellen's Best of Helpful Hints* (Warner 1979), *Mary Ellen's Best of Helpful Kitchen Hints* (Warner 1980), and *Mary Ellen's Best of Helpful Hints Book II* (Warner 1981), all by Mary Ellen Pinkham, provide a plethora of information on all aspects of homemaking. Students may be given a list of problems to solve, and they then may search for the answers in the library media center collection. Topics include cooking, fruits, spices, baking, freezing, entertaining, holidays, cleaning, children, outdoor barbecuing, trash, pests, handypersons, painting, landscaping, business, sewing, the car, the bathroom, etc.

Out Spot!

The home economics student may research in the library media center ways to remove stains and spots from a variety of fabrics and household surfaces. *Stain and Spot Removal Handbook* by the editors of *Consumer Guide* (Publications International 1981) is a fine example of an appropriate reference.

Miss Manners

Students may visit the library media center to research etiquette and manners in such references as *Emily Post's Book of Etiquette for Young People* (Funk & Wagnalls 1967); *Amy Vanderbilt's New Complete Book of Etiquette* (Doubleday 1963); and *Emily Post's Etiquette: The Blue Book of Social Usage* (Funk & Wagnalls 1965).

Commercial Videos

The library media center may purchase videos on any topic relating to the home economics field: styles of furniture; interior design and decorating; healthful snacks; grocery shopping; clothing care; consumer's shopping; etc.

VII. Industrial Arts

Woodworking Tour

The library media specialist may arrange for a tour of a woodworking business in the community. The industrial arts class may enjoy viewing a stair-making company, for example, or a furniture-making company. Or ask the business if you could make a videotape of the stair-making or furniture-making to bring back to the library media center. The practical aspect of watching woodworking procedures in the business world can be very beneficial.

Apprenticeship

The library media specialist can act as a liaison with a woodworking business by making a few phone calls inquiring whether it might be possible to engage a student in a small way, helping out and learning a few tips along the way. Those students who are ready to drop out of school or have little interest in academic subjects may greatly benefit, and it could even turn their attitudes around completely.

Woodworking Plans

The library media center may stock numerous books on woodworking projects including plans for clocks, shelves, toys, small pieces of furniture, games, etc. Students may check out books, or photocopy plans from books, vertical file materials and magazines such as *Home*

Industrial Arts Crossword I

ACROSS

1. A cutter's spindle that projects through a table and wood is passed over it.
5. This gives wood a thin, transparent coating.
7. Another name for California redwood.
8. The base of a branch enclosed in the stem from which it arises.
10. This is cut on table legs to allow them to appear more graceful.
13. Another name for Quebec pine.
15. Rough wood is _____.
17. A holding device for a bench usually placed to the left side against which work can be pressed when being planed.
18. What does red gum wood tend to do?
19. One use for hemlocks.
22. One of the heaviest softwoods. It is difficult to acquire a good finish.
23. What is beechwood used for?
26. The outer cortex of a tree.
27. This can be done on a jointer.
29. Used for face-planing, surfacing, jointing an edge or end, tapering, etc.
30. A lengthwise break or a big crack in a board.
31. One of the last steps before a wood project is completed.
32. There is a shade of purple in this wood.
33. This smooths wood.

DOWN

1. Elm wood resists _____.
2. Gaboon is considered a _____ wood.
3. When working with joints, what is used to get the bottom of a space level, but not necessarily smooth?
4. A plane with a bed 14 or 15 inches long.
6. The growth rings of a tree trunk are _____.
9. Nailing the end of one piece to the side of another piece of wood.
10. What wood secretes a resin?
11. This is a swamp tree.
12. Popular yellow is also known as _____ wood.
14. Casein glue is made from _____.
16. This wood is also known as whitewood.
19. This is an angle cut completely across the edge of a piece.
20. A lengthwise separation of wood.
21. The center of the tree trunk.
24. Chestnut looks and works like this hard wood.
25. What is outside the sapwood of a tree trunk?
27. What is basswood suitable for?
28. The teeth of a saw must be reshaped by _____.
31. A discoloration in the wood surface.
32. There is much more strength _____ the grain than across it.

Answers, p. 123.

Industrial Arts Crossword II

ACROSS

1. The hardest of the hardwoods.
3. A fence on a table saw is a guide that controls _____.
4. To make the teeth of a saw the same height.
5. Generally, glue is used for _____.
8. When a tenon is thinner than the mortise, and it has a shoulder on one side, if the opposite side is on the same level as the tenon side, it is a _____ tenon.
10. This is a guide used for cutting angles, that moves in a groove on the table saw, and carries a guide that is set to any angle.
13. A power saw with a continuous band.
14. A power saw with a short, stiff blade.
15. This wood is used for making plywood.
16. An angle.
17. The band saw has these everywhere except where it cuts.
18. What saw is most effective when cutting thin material?
20. This saw takes blades that fit through its handle, and can be exposed when needed.
22. Columbian pine is also known as _____.
23. Many saws have them to clear sawdust.

DOWN

1. Parana pine is found in _____.
2. The direction in which a band saw rotates makes it cut in which direction?
6. A round steel rod the same diameter as the bolts with a turned or filled taper at one end.
7. One can remove glue stains with a weak solution of this.
9. What kind of joints does one use in oblique joints?
11. A design is burned into the surface of the wood.
12. A power saw for making straight cuts.
13. The softest of the hardwoods.
17. What is urea-formaldehyde?
19. A table saw turned upside-down is a _____ saw.
20. The cut.
21. A planer is also called a _____.
22. There is no _____ control on a saber saw.

Answers, p. 123.

Mechanix. Projects may be displayed in the library media center upon completion.

Power Equipment Video

The library media center can be instrumental in the teaching of the safe use of power tools by videotaping the industrial arts instructor demonstrating the use of each machine. Or purchase a commercial video for use. The industrial arts department can borrow the video or the class can view it in the library media center.

Industrial Arts Gaming

The library media specialist can collaborate with the industrial arts instructor in producing a game. The game could be produced in the library media center to be used either in the library or back in the shop. The purpose of this game would be for the assimilation of information, and it could include almost any topic listed under industrial arts: for example, tools, safety, measurement, woods and materials, correct procedures, sketching and reading drawings, power equipment, etc.

Woodworking Careers

The library media center may be a great place to explore various careers available in the industrial arts field. The center will have numerous books, pamphlets, and directories in which students can locate further information on a specific career.

Decorating Wood

The industrial arts student may visit the library media center in order to research designs for decorating wood surfaces. Ideas for these designs may be found in art books, hobby and craft books, math books, etc.

Furniture Building

The library media center may house more elaborate plans in furniture building for the more advanced student. Our library media center contains plans for early American furniture, for example, and these are quite popular. Once again, the magazine section can be useful for this project.

Tools and Materials Video

Create another video illustrating hand tools, types of nails, types of woods, etc., with the collaboration of the industrial arts instructor. This can be used over and over again either in the shop or in the library media center.

Specific Subject Video

Tape a TV program or create a video on the making of a particular joint—a miter joint, for example. If several such types are made, the industrial arts teacher will then have a video library available in the library media center whenever the need arises.

Library Project

The industrial arts class may work on a needed project for the library media center. For example, they can build an extra bookcase that the library needs but cannot afford, or they can fix that wobbly dictionary stand.

Woodworking Hobbies

Students from the industrial arts class may visit the library media center in order to pursue hobbies related to the subject such as carving or whittling, or to locate plans for their own building creations outside of school assignments.

Wood Finishing

Students may locate information on wood finishes, materials, and procedures, not only in books, pamphlets, and reference tools, but in magazines.

Career Conversation

Invite a carpenter or other person involved in a woodworking career to the library media center in order to speak to students about life in the field.

TV Shows

Tape or purchase a few TV shows on woodworking such as "The New Yankee Workshop" and "This Old House." Inform the industrial arts instructor that the library media center has these available.

VIII. Mathematics

Mathematical Mart

Arrange to hold a "Math Mart" in the library. This may include pamphlets and information on careers using math. Addresses of associations may be made available. For example, careers in building houses or carpentry, engineering, math teaching, aviation, surveying, business, insurance, navigation, space travel and ballistics may be explored. Arrange to have one or two people come into the library to speak on a specific career in math. Also, include students' projects or posters showing how math is used in sports, cars, cooking, music, etc. The math classes may briefly visit the library media center to research these projects.

Polyhedron Perfection

For display in the library, the math class may construct geometrical solids, any of the seventy-five uniform polyhedra models, and also some of the stellated forms. Such books as *Polyhedron Models* by Magnus J. Wenninger (Cambridge University Press, 1971) and others may be used as a guide. The class may research these models in the library before they begin construction.

Math Fair

Students may do research in the school library media center in order to produce charts, booklets, or written reports as math projects

Mathematics Crossword I

ACROSS

3. ⩾ means _____ (in algebra).
5. A vector is a measure in which this is specified.
6. In sets and logic, U means _____.
7. The number of bits used to represent one letter in computing.
9. A logical argument showing a statement is true.
10. Another name for oscillation.
12. < means _____ (in geometry).
13. ⩽ means _____ than (in algebra).
15. In algebra, removing one of the unknowns in an equation.
17. A radical is an expression for a _____.
19. Gross includes the weight of the contents and its _____.
22. This is the mass of an object measured by inertia.
23. In sets and logic, V means _____.

DOWN

1. In algebra, what does ≡ mean?
2. What does ∧ mean in sets and logic?
4. A cosech is a _____ cosecant.
8. In geometry, ‖ means _____.
9. Coplanar means _____.
11. A null set is _____.
14. An erg is an old unit of _____.
16. In algebra, what does → mean?
18. The number into which the divisor is divided.
20. The lower side of a triangle in geometry.
21. What does a bisector do?

Answers, p. 124.

Mathematics Crossword II

ACROSS

2. In what subject is a parsec a unit?
5. Integers are the set of _____ numbers.
6. A carat is a unit used to measure _____.
7. Iteration solves problems by _____.
9. One number added together.
10. This is the distance from the center of a circle to a point on its circumference.
11. The value of a number that increases without any limit.
12. The meridian.
13. These are symbols used for measuring and counting.
14. This plane figure has four straight sides with both sides being parallel, and forming four right angles.
17. A rough calculation.
20. This is the distance around the edge of a plane.
21. A hyperbolic sine.

DOWN

1. An axis is a line in which the figure is _____.
3. The symbol k means _____.
4. What is a six-faced solid figure, each one being a parallelogram?
8. Thou means _____.
15. A method of making maps: _____ projection.
16. Cardinal numbers are used for _____.
18. This is an already proven theorem.
19. This number when added to another number does not change that number.

Answers, p. 124.

for a math fair. Topics may be anything of interest: history of mathematics; famous mathematicians; what is math; ancient computing methods such as the abacus, Napier's bones, or nomograph; ancient numbers; numeration systems; cryptography; graphing; measurement; statistics; probability and chance; number theory; different number bases; the metric system; computers and calculators; curve stitching and line design; math in income tax, banking, cooking, building a house; magic squares and puzzles; how to develop your own game; optical illusions; paper folding (origami); tangrams; solid geometry; quadrilaterals; volume and area; space travel; ballistics; different monetary systems; math in nature, in insurance, in art, in music, in science, in the automobile, in sports, in aviation, in navigation, in electronics, and on and on. The projects may be exhibited in the library media center.

Optical Illusion Show

The math class could come to the library to research the topic of optical illusions. Each student would construct a poster or exhibit, or perform an illusion for the class to see at the optical illusion show in the library at a later date.

Math Meet

The math class may visit the library media center in order to make up word problems using addition and multiplication operations or using percentages or decimals. Students will find these figures in the newspaper, magazine articles, or reference books such as the *World Almanac* and the *Guinness Book of World Records*. Word problems may be designed around sports scores, statistics, temperature records, precipitation percentages, Guinness world records, stock market information, etc. Students probably will need to have an example of such a word problem given to them. After students have designed one word problem, divide the class into two teams, giving half of the problems to each team. The winner is the team with the most correct answers.

Spherical Paragon

Students may research the library media center for references such as *Spherical Models* by Magnus J. Wenninger (Cambridge University Press 1979) in order to build, then display regular spherical models, semiregular spherical models, geodesic domes, and other models. Once again, these may be displayed in the library.

Math Applications

The math class may visit the library media center to research applications of math in specific careers. Each student may list as many careers as possible that include applications for mathematics, along with at least one way that math is utilized in that career. For example, a waitress must know how to make change, and a carpenter must know how to measure. Resources may include newspapers, magazines, career books, occupational guides and pamphlets from the vertical file.

Shopping Spree

Each student of the math class may be given a specific amount of make-believe money. Students will be instructed that they are to "spend" the money wisely by "shopping" in the newspapers and magazines in the library media center. They must spend all their money without going over the amount, and must shop for quality and lowest price. Sales tax should be calculated also. Students may be divided up into groups, some being responsible for handling grocery items, some cars, some houses, some entertainment items such as stereos, some clothing, etc.

Newspaper Math

The math class can locate in the library media center examples of fractions, decimals, ratios, percentages, and averages in the newspapers. They may be instructed to find as many references to the above as possible. The instructor may ask them how these articles in the newspaper could be written without any references to math.

History of Math Book

Students of the math class may utilize the library media center by researching the history of mathematics and mathematicians. Suggested topics: Egyptian and Phoenician math; Greek math; Byzantine math; primitive arithmetic and numerous systems of numeration; math of the Middle Ages and the Renaissance; math in the time of the Arabs; and the more modern math from Descartes. Upon researching a topic, each student could be responsible for creating his own "book." These books can be exhibited in the library.

Double Tangrams

Students from the math class may utilize the library media center to locate photos and illustrations or stories from which they can construct double tangrams. A single tangram consists of seven parts, and can be arranged in various ways to make a design. The double tangrams make use of two single tangrams together. The class may design one picture of animals, cars, etc., or tell a story with a group of tangrams. These may be exhibited.

Geometric Forms

The math class may do research in the library media center for math books displaying patterns and designs of geometry. There are numerous sources; one is *Arabic Geometrical Pattern and Design* by J. Bourgoin (Dover 1973). Students may draw patterns and designs or make models of these to display.

Graphing

The math class may visit the library media center in order to research topics in reference books such *World Almanac*, newspapers, and magazines, and may then make a graph indicating statistical activity related to that topic. For instance, a student may research and then graph the rise and decline of temperatures for a specific season or for a two week period. Numerous topics could be explored and graphed.

Origami

The math class may visit the library in order to explore books on origami or paper folding, and also to find illustrations of shapes to duplicate. These may be suspended from the ceiling by wire, and would make a great exhibit anywhere.

Sports Math

The math class may research in the library sports records in various reference books, magazines, and newspapers. One reference is *The Encyclopedia of Sports* by Frank Menke (A.S. Barnes 1969). Statistics, such as comparisons of how individual teams did in a specific sport during a season, could then be computed by averages, percentages, ratios, decimals, charts or graphs.

IX. Microcomputers

Computer Compulsion

Students can make designs on the computers in computer class, or in the library media center. These designs may be the students' original creations or copied from books in the library. They may be displayed in the library, with the most intricate or creative design winning a prize.

Computer News

Students may investigate computer news in the newspaper and magazine articles in the library media center. Any article regarding computers may be researched, and students may then write summaries.

Computer Games

Students may come to the library media center in order to research computer game books such as *Invent Your Own Computer Games* by Fred D'Ignazio (D'Ignazio 1983), and other books that will provide examples of games and instruct in game design techniques. Students may then create their own games: sports games, strategy games, number games, word games, adventure games, board games. The game should be short and simple with the program being no longer than 20 or 30 lines, and each line should have one or few commands, so that the programs may be typed into the computer in a half-hour or less. Students may come to the library media center in order to work on the computer terminals.

Computer Poetry

Students from the computer class may locate sixteenth, seventeenth, or eighteenth century poems in the library media center in the poetry section. Then, using a computer equipped with a good word processing program, they may rearrange, delete, add to, and change the lines of each poem so that one would think that the poem was being composed today in today's language. Or the students can program the computer to make up a poem, free-verse without rhyme. This can be done by thinking of and keying in all the words that one wishes to include in the poem in the form of a list. Students can write a program that would allow the computer to randomly choose words. Or they may set up a form which includes where the subjects and verbs will go, etc.

Computer Applications

Students may visit the library to research how computers may be utilized in the various professions: government and business, education, medicine, science, engineering and industry, law enforcement, personal affairs, etc. They may write up reports or make posters to be exhibited.

Computer Poster

Use the computer to design posters or banners for upcoming school functions: spirit week activities, school dances, sports games and concerts. Students may design these by checking on these programs in the school library media center's computer section.

Computer Cryptography

Students using the media center may research ways to write a program which transforms an original program into nonsense in order to

Microcomputers Crossword I

ACROSS

1. "A symbol written between two operands and specifying the operation to be performed."
3. This prevents _____ from entering a connector.
5. "A microprocessor with peripheral unit interfaces, allowing a complete computing system."
8. A file is "an organized collection of related _____."
10. To pull is "to remove an element from a _____."
12. To log is "to record events in _____ sequence."
13. Deck means _____.
16. CRT is an abbreviation for _____.
17. "Synonymous with instruction."
19. "A group of adjacent binary digits operated on as one unit."
22. An acoustic coupler is a device using a _____.
24. UV means _____.
25. Garbage is "meaningless and unwanted _____."
26. "A group of items which itself belongs to a larger group."

DOWN

1. "Synonymous with instruction."
2. Not-both means _____.
4. "A unit of work organized to be processed by a computer."
6. "An action defined by a single instruction."
7. Delete means to _____.
9. Programs.
11. "The diagrammatic representation of a flow."
14. A bug is a _____.
15. A symbol is a _____.
18. RO means _____.
19. "A contraction of binary digits."
20. Boolean logic is "synonymous with Boolean _____."
21. Memory capacity is "the number of units of data that can be stored in memory, expressed as the number of _____ available."
23. Flip-flop means _____.

Answers, pp. 124–25.

Microcomputers Crossword II

ACROSS

1. A tube is a _____.
3. A head _____ data.
6. To quiesce means to reject new jobs in this system.
8. Edit routine means _____.
11. K is an abbreviation for _____.
12. An accordion is a printed circuit connector.
13. What function does an inverter perform?
17. A head _____ data.
19. Electrical tough pitch is a grade of _____.
20. The abbreviation for hexidecimal notation.
21. A deque is a double-ended _____.
23. Cell means _____ cell.
26. Searching for.
27. Analog computer is contrasted to _____ computer.
28. B-store means _____.
29. A quad is four insulated _____ twisted together.
30. On-line means under the control of a central _____.

DOWN

1. Lap is "to smooth the surface of a wafer of _____."
2. A test bed is used for _____ testing.
4. RAM is an acronym for _____.
5. A head _____ data.
7. The octal number system uses _____ as a base.
9. Any random-access storage device which uses magnetic tape.
10. A cursor may be seen on a _____ display.
14. And gate means _____.
15. What is a carry?
16. An adder can perform _____.
18. Chapter means _____.
22. An algorithm is a series of _____.
24. Tera means one million _____.
25. A wafer is a slice from a _____ ingot.

Answers, p. 125.

protect anyone from reading it. Students will explore ways to make a cipher or a precise list of steps to follow that will transform their program.

Computer Art

The computer class may research the media center's photographs, illustrations, and designs in order to get ideas to use for their own computer artworks. They will likewise locate computer literature on techniques for "painting" pictures using their computers.

Computer Music

The students of the computer class can visit the school library media center to investigate how a computer makes music, and how to write a music program. Also, they may investigate how to make all kinds of sound effects.

Building Computer Models

Students may visit the library media center in order to research the dozens of excellent books that can teach students how to build models, not out of wood and glue, but on the computer screen.

Computer History

The computer class can utilize the library to research the history of computers, the beginning of our modern day microcomputers, the programming language, and the types of computers that are available today.

Computer Home Applications

In the library media center, students may research the home applications of using a computer, such as programs for checkbook balancing, monthly accounts payable, food, entertainment, savings, clothing budget, meal planning and inventory.

Computer Vocabulary

The computer students can look up computer definitions in the library media center as their assignment for computer class.

Confidential Codes

This secret code exercise may be used in conjunction with the computer class. Students will visit the library in order to locate a paragraph from a book, a short newspaper column, a poem, or whatever, and translate this into binary code. Students will exchange papers to decipher the codes. The secret or confidential code is in base 2, which is the binary code. The idea is for students to punch holes in graph paper or adding machine tape to make a secret message.

The letters of the alphabet are indicated as a row of holes and spaces. Each row may have as many as five holes or none at all. Values indicated by each hole are as follows:

	2	2	2	2	2
	16	8	4	2	1
First row	0		0		
Second row		0	0	0	0
Third row		0	0		0

A	B	C	D	E	F	G	H	I	J	K	L	M	N
1	2	3	4	5	6	7	8	9	10	11	12	13	14

O	P	Q	R	S	T	U	V	W	X	Y	Z
15	16	17	18	19	20	21	22	23	24	25	26

The above secret code spells TOM.

Computer Fun

Students have a sign-up to use the computers in our library media center, and they can come to use them just for plain fun to do whatever they wish, or to do homework assignments.

X. Music

Folksongs U.S.A.

The music class may visit the library media center in order to research the various themes, types, styles and tunes of American folksongs. *The 111 Best of American Ballads: Folk Song U.S.A.* by Alan Lomax, ed., is a good example of an appropriate reference. Each student may be assigned a specific theme or type of folksong as well as a specific area of the country to research.

Pop Music

Music students may investigate the history of pop music from the turn of the century, examining ways in which this music distinctly reflects changes in American society and life styles. Students can research jazz in the '20s; swing in the '30s; the "sing" era of the '40s; rock 'n' roll of the '50s; folk music of the '60s; hard-rock sound of the '70s; and the varied sounds of the '80s including the country sound.

Jazz

The library media center may house references on jazz which the music class may investigate. They may research the basic elements of this form of music, its rhythms, forms and harmonies, and the vital role of improvisation, etc. Various styles could be explored such as New Orleans, Dixieland, blues, bop, progressive, and the free jazz of today.

Music Crossword I: Instruments

ACROSS

3. A low-sounding woodwind with a single reed.
7. A percussion instrument; a wooden hoop with metal discs that jingle.
8. A percussion instrument arranged like a piano with a hollow tube; a set of wooden bars.
9. A stringed instrument of 47 strings and 7 foot pedals.
10. Another word for a tam-tam.
12. A stringed instrument held between the knees with a low, rich mellow sound.
13. A small harpsichord of the 16th and 17th century.
14. A harpsichord in a small four- or five-sided case.
16. A stringed instrument called the pianoforte.
17. This is also called timpani.
21. The modern lute with a pear shape.
23. Also known as the klavier.
24. A brass wind instrument with a slide.

DOWN

1. A brass wind with the lowest pitch.
2. The largest of the drums.
4. This instrument has the deepest voice of the orchestra.
5. Similar to the glockenspiel, but also has wooden resonators.
6. Metal plates clashed together.
10. A percussion instrument which is a line of steel bars like a piano, played with wooden hammers.
11. An accordion-like, free-reed instrument that is six-sided with buttons.
15. A low-pitched brass wind having a cup mouthpiece and valve.
18. A woodwind with one reed.
19. A four-stringed Hawaiian instrument.
20. A small drum with wire or gut stretched across it; makes a rattling sound.
22. An ancient harp.

Answers, p. 125.

Music Crossword II

ACROSS

2. Simile.
4. Unaccompanied choral singing.
6. Piano means _____.
7. Barcarole comes from this word.
10. Unaccompanied secular choral music in contrapuntal style.
11. A rhapsody is a _____.
12. Loud.
15. Pomposo means _____.
18. Plucking.
19. A gradual dying away on an ending.
20. A mordent is a musical _____.
23. Sweet and soft.
25. Little.
29. Soft pedal.
31. Sad.
32. Sharply detached.
34. A vertical line connected to the head of a note.
35. A forerunner of the piano.

DOWN

1. A stately dance of the 16th, 17th, and 18th centuries which is in slow triple time.
2. Tristo means _____.
3. Gradually growing slower.
5. Slowly, but faster than largo.
7. With spirit, bold.
8. A composition for two performers.
9. Molto means _____.
13. A stringed instrument that begins with z, with a flat wooden sound box.
14. Half or medium.
16. A work.
17. Dissonance is _____.
21. Duple time means _____ beats to the measure.
22. A light opera.
24. Pitch is the exact _____ of a sound in a range of tones.
26. Another name for timpani.
27. Running the fingers across the keys.
28. P is an abbreviation for _____.
30. Tutti means _____.
33. A percussion instrument; used singly or in pairs.

Answers, p. 126.

Jazz musicians may be explored: Louis Armstrong, Charlie Parker, Billie Holiday, John Coltrane, Miles Davis and others.

Musician's Visit

Arrange for a local musician from the local symphony to visit the library media center. Invite the music classes to hear what it is like to play professionally in an orchestra, how many years one must take lessons, and how long one must practice each day. Perhaps the musician could give a short demonstration.

Great Excerpts

The music class may always have available to them recordings or cassettes of excerpts from the world's greatest music. Students may listen to music with earphones in the media center if there is no time in the music room.

Folk Instruments

The music class may come to the library in order to research various folk instruments, such as the fiddle, the banjo, the guitar, the ukulele, the mandolin, the zither, the Jew's harp, the bagpipe, the mouth organ, the accordion, and others. The class may write short reports on these instruments.

Orchestra

Likewise, the class may come to the media center to explore the instruments of the symphony orchestra. The woodwinds, percussion instruments, strings, and brass instruments may be researched, and reported on.

Field Trips

The library media specialist may locate listings of local concerts and musical theater happenings, and may make these available to the music instructor. Also, special TV or radio concerts or music programs may be taped for the class, and made available to the class at a later date.

Musical Terms

Students may be asked to look up definitions of musical terms in the library's references. Books such as *Music Dictionary* by Marilyn Kornreich Davis (Doubleday 1956) and many, many other sources can be used.

Readers' Guide

The *Abridged Readers' Guide to Periodical Literature* contains countless references to magazine articles in the field of music. One assignment students find interesting is to locate several articles about rock music, and write summaries of their findings.

American Music

Music forms of America—folk, jazz, rock, early Black music, songs of slavery, blues and boogie woogie, etc.—may be explored by listening to examples on earphones, and by researching books and magazines. Students may select examples of a specific type of music to report on, and they may put together a concert for the class by borrowing recordings from the media center.

Music Throughout the World

Broader musical horizons may be explored: music in Bali; Indian classical music; African music; Japanese music; etc. Students may listen to music on earphones, do research from books and magazine articles, and learn of upcoming concerts in the library.

Music History

The music class may explore music history, from the beginnings of music to modern twentieth century styles. How music came to be; music of ancient nations (Egypt, Assyria, the Hebrews, the Greeks and Romans); music of the Orientals or the Arabs; church music; troubadours and minnesingers to folk music; motets and madrigals of the fifteenth and sixteenth centuries; oratorio and opera; music in England and France; harpsichord composers; organ music; tone poets; and many more topics under the history of music may be explored. Students may research, and compose a music book on their particular topic.

Music Theory

The music instructor may request that the class visit the library media center in order to explore how the composer works in his art form: notes, scales and keys, rhythm, melody, harmony, counterpoint. Students may choose a specific piece of music from the library collection to study.

Composers

Once again, the library media center houses various reference tools in the field of music, many dealing solely with composers. For example, *Biographical Dictionary of American Music* by Charles Claghorn (Parker 1973); *Popular American Composers* by David Ewen (Wilson 1962); *Composers Since 1900* by David Ewen (Wilson 1981); *Great Composers 1300–1900* by David Ewen (Wilson 1966); *Composers Since 1900* by David Ewen (Wilson 1981); and numerous other references and general encyclopedias. The music student may research composers for papers and assignments.

XI. Physical Education

Demonstration Video

A video can be made by the media department of the proper techniques of playing a sport. This video can be shown to the physical education classes in the library media center. Videos can be made using the physical education classes. Also, members of the ski club, bicycling club, or hiking club may demonstrate techniques of their sports. These videos can be utilized for years to come.

Exercise Video

Commercial exercise videos with aerobics and calisthenics may be obtained by the library and utilized by the physical education department.

Sports Banquet

The library media center houses countless books on sports in the general collection, as well as reference books, magazines and newspapers. The physical education class may be scheduled to come to the library for a "sports banquet." Each table of the library could feature a separate sport. A few magazine articles, rules of the game, and explanations of basic techniques could be photocopied for students.

Physical Education Crossword I

ACROSS

2. What are the Maccabiah games similar to?
6. A player occupying the middle position.
8. A riposte is a _____ after a parry.
12. The opposite of forehand.
13. What is korfball similar to?
16. This is used instead of gasoline in some racing engines.
18. A line running the width and at both ends of a soccer field.
19. A lepper is a horse competing in _____.
20. To overcome an opponent's pass, and gain possession of a ball.
22. Pea is a term used in _____.
23. A K valve is used in _____.

DOWN

1. In what sport is expansion bolt used?
3. Another name for boccino.
4. "Major" is the abbreviated form of "major _____."
5. A mark.
7. Lifting in volleyball is a _____.
9. A KO in boxing is a _____.
10. In motor racing, an igniter is highly volatile _____ that is added to a slow-burning fuel.
11. A match that ends by a tie.
14. A foldboat is a collapsible _____.
15. Curling resembles _____.
17. This stores fishing line.
19. What is a PA?
21. What is Italian pursuit?

Answers, p. 126.

Physical Education
Crossword II: Sports

ACROSS

1. The shape of a billiard table.
4. Love is a score of _____.
7. A runner on a cross-country team.
9. In boxing, the 145 and later 147 pound champions are called _____.
11. The neutral zone of an ice hockey rink.
15. The number one autumn sport of the United States.
16. The mother-in-law pin in bowling.
17. In bowling, the act of snapping the fingers up quickly when the ball is released to give it spin.
20. In what sport is the "King's cup" given?
22. What determines class among race horses?
23. In football, to carry the ball in a running play is to _____.
25. Another name for billiards.
26. In cricket, what are placed 66 feet apart?
30. This sport is played on ice by a team of six players.
32. How many yards is an American football endzone?

DOWN

1. Played with an oval ball with H-shaped goals on a rectangular field.
2. A game played on the lawn with a mallet.
3. What is a billiard table covered with?
5. These games are held every 4 years in a different country.
6. In volleyball, how many times may a ball be batted by one team before it must be sent across the net?
8. How many holes is a round of golf?
10. Similar to baseball, but played on a smaller field using a larger ball.
11. These are systematic rhythmic body exercises without equipment.
12. A homerun in baseball.
13. In tennis, the head frame is usually _____.
14. Where soccer originated.
18. When the score is love-20, the game is _____.
19. A sidestroke movement in swimming, if used in the breast stroke, may result in _____.
21. How many inches high is the center of the mound in baseball?
22. In what sport does one use bindings and poles?
24. Near side is the left side of a _____.
27. This is the art of self-defense with kicks and punches.
28. What is used in curling?
29. A kick made by dropping the ball, and kicking it as it bounces.
31. A type of canoe.

Answers, p. 127.

Cheerleading

A video of a demonstration of cheerleading techniques may also be made by the library media center, and used for years to come by the cheerleading coach.

Dance

The girls' physical education class may visit the library media center in order to research various types of dance, particularly ballet. The librarian can invite a local dance teacher for a brief visit to the school. Students interested in pursuing a career in dance or having their own dance studio may enjoy this activity.

Sports Briefs

Students of the physical education class can do research on various sports in the *New York Times Encyclopedia of Sports,* edited by Gene Brown (Arno/Grolier 1979), which contains newspaper articles on baseball; football; basketball; track and field; golf; tennis; boxing; soccer; hockey; skating; skiing; shooting; soaring; rugby; polo; mountain climbing; hunting; fishing; bicycling; bullfighting; squash; judo; jiu-jitsu; karate; equestrianism; gymnastics; fencing; bowling; billiards; badminton; water sports; water skiing; swimming and diving; boating; surfing; yachting; horse racing; and auto racing.

"Jeopardy" — Physical Education

This activity is borrowed from the popular TV show, and may inspire participation from all the subjects in the curriculum including physical education. Students can be given a list of questions and topics used for the actual game, and they would come to the library media center with their class prior to this game in order to research the answers. They may come to the library more than once to research the rules for baseball, football, volleyball, tennis, etc. Five categories of topics would be given. The game could be a battle among three members of a class, with new students coming in to challenge each time one of the three is a winner. A student would receive one point for each correct answer, and one point would be deducted from his score for each incorrect answer.

Physical Conditioning

The physical education classes may come to the library to research the physical requirements needed for various careers.

Gaming — Physical Education

In cooperation with the physical education instructor, prepare a board game or other such game that would involve students in the assimilation of information on some aspects of playing sports or physical conditioning. The class may come to the library media center or the game could be checked out.

Local and TV Games

Videotape portions of an important TV game or a local game, and have this available for the physical education department. Post important upcoming games for after school field trips or for TV viewing.

Drugs in Sports

The problem of drugs in sports may be explored: the reasons for their use, the occurrence, and the consequences. The *Readers' Guide* should provide many citations of current articles on the topic.

Student Video

Videotape the students of the physical education class in action playing a sport. The physical education instructor may use this as a tool to point out correct and incorrect techniques.

Sports Marathon

Students in the physical education class may be given a list of questions to research in the library media center. A contest of cross-questions between two teams can then be held with the winning team giving the most correct answers. Or the students who give incorrect answers may be deleted from the team, and the one student remaining wins for that team.

Twentieth Century Sports

Students may research the recent political and commercial pressures affecting athletes: drugs, spectator violence, and the terrific financial rewards that have degraded the traditional ideas of sportsmanship. Sports in the twentieth century may be explored in the library media center, compared to what was the traditional concept of sports.

Hero Worship

Students may explore statistics and records of athletes who have been inducted into the Hall of Fame, or other great athletes. Several references may be consulted.

XII. Science

Sound Show

The science class will come to the library media center to research experiments in sound. After each student locates one experiment to perform, and takes notes or has it photocopied, he or she prepares the experiment in order to perform it at a later date for the class, either in the library or back in the classroom.

Nuclear Energy Council Meeting

Students from the science class will visit the library media center to research the nuclear power controversy. Specialized reference books, the general collection, and pamphlets and booklets from the vertical file may provide plenty of information. Students will learn about how electricity is generated using nuclear energy; the benefits and drawbacks of nuclear power; how decisions are made in society; and how information must be gathered and evaluated before sound decisions can be made on the use of nuclear power. Hold a "public meeting" with students discussing whether to build a nuclear reactor in their community or an imaginary community. Before researching this decision in the library, students will be assigned as witnesses or council members. Each witness must give a five to ten minute presentation to the council, as well as answer questions from the council members. Each council member must ask the witnesses five questions and listen to the witness presentation. The council will then present their decision and their reasons for it.

Science Crossword I: Aquariums

ACROSS

1. What is collargol used for on fish?
5. A chemical that can soften hard water.
6. This is necessary in an aquarium with rooted plants.
7. A diffusion is a spontaneous _____ of substances.
9. Aquariums are made watertight by a special _____.
10. Warmer water on top, cooler water below.
14. Fungus is caused by _____.
16. The reason for green water in an aquarium.
21. One remedy for green water is to cover the aquarium from _____.
22. What is gray water a sign of?
25. Another method of curing green water is to change the _____.
26. This is needed in the marine aquarium.

DOWN

2. Another word for skin.
3. One reason to condition water is to remove _____ gas.
4. Blackened sand or gravel should be removed with a _____.
8. Flukes are a _____ of the gills.
11. What is menhaden?
12. Treating water is called _____.
13. Water is composed of hydrogen and _____.
15. Green water is caused by too much _____.
17. Sight is important for reproduction and _____ of fish.
18. One of the commonest water bacteria.
19. The bottoms of aquariums are made up of glass or _____.
20. Where do physailia come from?
23. The most desirable of live foods for aquarium fish.
24. DH is the measure of the _____ dissolved in the water.

Answers, p. 127.

Science Crossword II

ACROSS

3. DC is an abbreviation for _____.
6. A micropyle is an _____ in the seed coat.
7. Diageotropism is a tendency of roots and tree branches to grow at this type of angle.
9. What does intrusive describe?
10. This instrument measures absolute humidity of air or gas.
11. Sidereal time is time in regard to the _____.
12. This device measures small distances.
14. This device bombards atomic nuclei.
17. This instrument enlarges objects when viewing through it.
18. A stator is a stationary _____ of an electrical generator.
19. To gel means to _____.
21. In astronomy, this is a change in the position of a close celestial body.
23. In chemistry, friable refers to a substance that can easily be made into a

   _____.
24. Dextrose is a simple _____.
25. A flux is a substance that aids in _____.

DOWN

1. This is the time it takes the earth to make one trip around the sun.
2. What color is cinnabar?
4. When seen through a lens, this is an apparent enlargement.
5. This refers to an uncombined state of an element in chemistry.
6. In biology, a category of related plants or animals.
8. What is chyme?
10. This is a reaction of water with a compound resulting in a weak acid.
13. This is a tropical wind system in which wind blows from sea to land for approximately six months, and from land to sea for the following six months.
15. What is produced when bituminous coal is distilled?
16. A change in direction of light waves.
17. The middle layer of cells in an animal embryo.
20. A standard solution is usually a _____ solution.
22. What does the dura mater enclose?

Answers, p. 128.

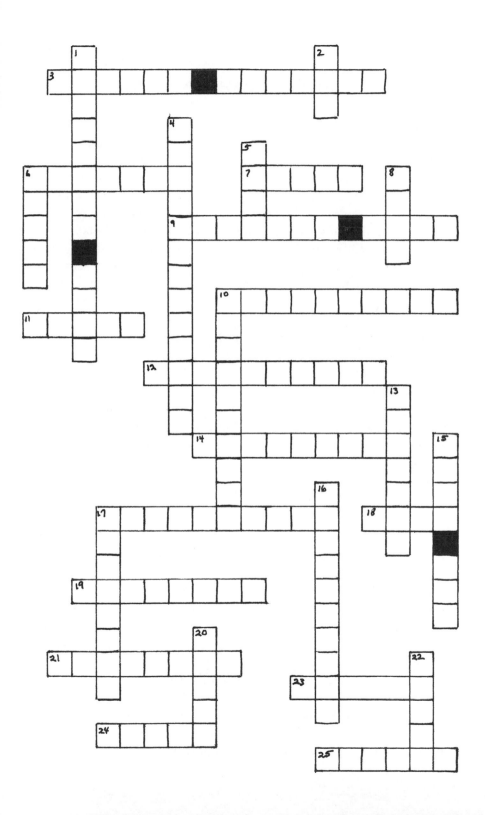

Patterns from Nature

In references in the library media center, the science students will locate photographs of various patterns in nature, such as ferns, snowflakes, galaxies, crystals, tortoise shells, branching trees, etc. Upon locating photos, and photocopying or hand-copying these, they are then to explain the laws of science governing these patterns such as the laws of flow, stress, turbulence, least effort, surface tension, close packing or whatever applies to the photograph. There are various themes or patterns that repeat themselves in nature, such as spirals, branching patterns, explosions, and meanders; the science student will research and explain how each evolved according to the laws of science.

Futuristic Exploration

Science students may explore and research science in the twentieth century and beyond. One excellent reference is the encyclopedia set *Twentieth Century* by A.J.P. Taylor, editor-in-chief (Purnell Reference 1979). There are numerous other resources. Students must research advances likely to be made in the twenty-first century.

Drug Delirium

The living skills, health education, or science class may come to the library to research various drugs, and their ill effects. Each student will concentrate on one specific drug, such as cocaine, marijuana, hashish, heroin, amphetamines, alcohol, caffeine or nicotine. More than one student may research the same drug. Students will design anti-drug posters and display them throughout the school and in the library.

Nature Walk

After going on a nature walk, collecting specimens of plants, leaves, and flowers, the science class will research their finds in the library media center, exploring the phyla and descriptions.

Analytical Key

Upon being given a list of perhaps ten animals, the science student will explore the numerous characteristics of each animal in order to find at least three similarities among succeeding animals on the list. For example, animal #1, the tiger, has fangs; animal #2, the rattlesnake, has fangs; etc.

Science Careers

Students may come to the library media center to research careers in all areas of science: biology and the life sciences; psychology; medicine; astronomy; chemistry; physics; space exploration; etc. Students will locate as many careers as they can on each branch of science while noting the educational background one must pursue for each career. Students may also locate addresses of associations to seek further information on careers.

TV Productions

Videotape TV productions on scientific subjects including the National Geographic Specials, Omni, Odyssey, the PBS productions of NOVA, and others. Make these available to the science classes.

Science in the News

The science class may collect newspaper headlines and articles of scientific terms, events, and people involved in science. Students may research the history of scientific events, and how science and technological developments have changed our life. They may predict what future discoveries might be.

Environmental Problems

The science class may locate newspaper and magazine articles plus materials in the general and reference collection that have to do with environmental problems: pollution, acid rain, nuclear energy accidents, recycling, etc. They may write papers stating what problems exist, why, what organizations or people are involved with these problems, and what is being done to solve the problems, if anything.

Microscopic Worlds

Students will be given a list of items, such as bacteria, viruses, protozoa, amoebas, flagellates, ciliates, sporozoa, algae and fungi, and yeasts, of which they must find microscopic photos in the library media center.

How-To

Students may write "how-to" articles on scientific topics of interest, keeping in mind the importance of sequence as they write. They may consult magazine articles located by using the *Readers' Guide*, newspaper articles, and science references in the reference and general collection. Charts and illustrations may enhance the content of the articles.

Science in Our Life

Students may visit the school library media center in order to explore the role science plays in our everyday life. Students may look through magazines, newspapers, reference books, and the general collection to find references to indicate that science is with us. For example, frozen food advertisements call attention to the fact that science gave us the know-how to freeze and preserve foods.

History of Science

Science students can utilize the school library media center by researching an historical development of science. Study, for example, how man fought off disease from the beginning of time to now, and project possible methods of the future; or how man clothed himself from the beginning of time to now, and the related technological developments.

Answers

Art Crossword I

ACROSS

3. Charcoal
5. Kiln
7. Chiaroscuro
9. Balsa wood
11. Gray
13. Linseed oil
15. Mingling
17. Relief
18. Rice
20. Impressionism
23. Portraits
26. Rough
27. Delacroix

DOWN

1. Batik
2. Woodcuts
4. Black
6. Gray
8. Matisse
10. Horizon
11. Grisaille
12. Meet
14. Alla prima
16. Germany
18. Rembrandt
19. Pop art
21. Retarders
22. Arp
24. Renoir
25. Glue

Art Crossword II

ACROSS

4. Dots
6. Renoir
8. Serigraphy
10. Wax
12. Calligraphy
14. Oil
15. Gouache
16. Impasto

17. Hue
19. Flemish
20. Seurat
22. Paris
24. Origami
25. Clay
27. Green
28. El Greco
29. Neoclassicism
30. Pureness

DOWN

1. Fresco
2. Picasso
3. Baroque
5. Tzara
7. Primary
9. Picasso
11. Michelangelo

12. Cezanne
13. Impressionism
15. Gesso
18. Italy
21. Easel
23. Rococo
24. Opaque
26. Mural

English Crossword I

ACROSS

1. Thomas Carlyle
3. John Byron
6. John Galsworthy
10. Henry Longfellow
12. Henry Clay
14. Mark Twain

DOWN

2. Marshall McLuhan
4. Arthur Guiterman
5. Horatio Nelson
7. Paul Brooks
8. Stephen Foster
9. William Walsh
11. James Agee
13. Edward Lear

English Crossword II: Thesaurus

ACROSS

2. Lucrative
5. Ghostly
10. Infect
11. Versatile
12. Dominate
14. Failing
17. Sophisticated
19. Droll
20. Dandy
21. Fistfight
23. Vernal
26. Open
29. Daydreamer
31. Relaxing

DOWN

1. Single-mindedness
3. Capsize
4. Calculated
6. Reticent
7. Rooted
8. Artificial
9. Ovation
13. Disorganized
15. Indolent
16. Notorious
18. Cool
22. Flashy
24. Spare
25. Yield
27. Nomad
28. Brave
30. Apex

English Crossword III: *Dracula*

ACROSS

1. Journal
6. Water
7. Dracula
9. Renfield
10. Heart
12. Smoke
14. Wolf
17. Mina Murray
19. Demeter
21. Invited
25. Elements
27. Orphan
28. Carpathian
30. Younger
33. Mirror
34. Danelles
35. Sleepwalks
36. Rose

DOWN

1. Jonathan Harper
2. Undead
3. Canine
4. Swales
5. Trance
8. Arthur
11. Nosferatu
13. Quincey
14. Whitby
15. Superstitions
16. Crucifix
18. Van Helsing
20. Die
22. Varna
23. Daylight
24. Bloofer Lady
26. Mystery
29. Animals
31. Prison
32. Garlic
35. Sea

English Crossword IV: *The Pearl*

ACROSS

2. Village
4. Christian
6. Juana
7. Hut
9. Mat
12. Animal
14. Pearl buyers
15. Dawn
16. Coyotito
17. Kills
19. Doctor
20. Masculine
22. Paste
24. Motifs
27. Tracker
29. Four
30. Poultice
32. Indian
33. Dies
35. Novella
36. Night
37. Symbols

DOWN

1. Family
3. Equal
5. Tomas
8. Buyers
10. Sell
11. Single
13. Apolonia
16. Caves

17. Kino
18. Priest
21. Loreto
23. Howl
25. Scorpion
26. Three
28. Gate
31. Windy
34. Ant

English Crossword V: *The Hobbit*

ACROSS

2. Stone
4. Baggins
6. Gold
7. Exotic
8. Adventure
9. Dwarf
11. Dismiss
13. Gollum
14. Ponies
15. Barrels
16. No
18. Power
22. Reconciled
26. Shire
27. Riddles
28. Key
29. Middle Earth
34. Hobbits
35. Sleep
36. Arkenstone

DOWN

1. Pipe
3. Thorin
4. Burrow
5. Wizard
9. Dragon
10. Bombur
12. Spider
17. Oakenshield
19. Odd
20. Elrond
21. Five armies
23. Dies
24. Thrush
25. Metal
30. Lake-Town
31. Goblin
32. Thirteen
33. Spot

English Crossword VI: *Moby Dick*

ACROSS

1. Ishmael
3. Forehead
5. Gam
6. Steelkilt
9. Escapes
11. Father Mapple
13. Charts

14. Sick
15. Daggoo
17. Son
19. Gray
21. Whalemen's
23. Pip
25. Epic
26. Starbuck

DOWN

2. Massachusetts
3. Flask
4. Drama
5. Gabriel
7. Evil
8. Jaw

10. Queequeg
11. Fleece
12. East Indians
16. Ahab
18. Nantucket
20. Pacific
22. Mayhew
24. Fire

English Crossword VII: *Kidnapped*

ACROSS

3. David Balfour
5. Maclean
7. Laird
9. Fox
10. Scotland
11. Rents
12. Elder
16. Maccoll
20. Essendean
21. House
23. Shuan
25. Sheamus
27. Stuart
29. Rest
31. Jennet
32. Ross of Mull

DOWN

1. Macpherson
2. Duncan
4. Dialect
6. Alexander
8. Ransome
13. Roy
14. Corrynakiegh
15. Henderland
17. Linnhe
18. Ardshiel
19. Rankeillor
22. Thompson
24. Campbells
26. Silver
28. Twins
30. Moor

Foreign Language Crossword I

ACROSS

1. Myndighet
4. Bilet
6. Krochmal
8. Droga
11. Eraro
12. Amarillo
13. Hari Lattie
17. Gamal
19. Saai
20. Ski
21. Grat

22. Knoblauch
26. Oo
29. Mitro
30. Kwiecien
31. Opettaja

DOWN

1. Mbegu za mti cacao
2. Nouqta
3. Hukkua
4. Bon marché
5. Podatek
7. San
9. Polagano

10. Kravata
14. Jatszik
15. Industrie
18. Lexikon
23. Toa
24. Ac
25. Chimie
27. Kohdata
28. Vie

Foreign Language Crossword II

ACROSS

3. Raccommoder
6. Nichoir
8. Noix
9. Envasement
10. Vedette
11. Jeu
14. Encens
15. Reine
18. Poussette
19. Oser
21. Cabinet
22. Dépouiller
23. Abouchement
25. Renfrogné
30. Pétillant
32. Remedy
33. Limitrophe
35. Mechanic

DOWN

1. Bronchement
2. Tignonner
4. Évidemment
5. Expatriate
7. Compte
12. Gribouille
13. Père
16. Souverain
17. Peu
20. Çà
24. Rejoindre
25. Ramaigrir
26. Friperie
27. Né
28. Fune
29. Femme
31. Probant
34. Pied

Guidance Crossword I

ACROSS

3. Race car driver
4. Taxidermist
6. Surveyor
8. Waitress
9. Banker
10. Anthropologist
13. Pediatrician
14. Nursing
15. Podiatrist
18. Baker
19. Priest

DOWN

1. Teacher
2. Librarian
5. Drama coach
7. Reporter
11. Hospital orderly
12. Telephone operator
16. Architect
17. Sculptor

Guidance Crossword II

ACROSS

2. Communication
8. Honesty
11. Anger
12. Read
14. Family
15. Excel
18. Introvert
19. Time
23. Drugs
24. Attitudes
25. Curfews
26. Fear
28. Place
29. Passive

DOWN

1. Positive
3. Moods
4. Listener
5. Agree
6. Do things
7. Life
9. No
10. Tactful
13. Extrovert
16. Active
17. Body language
20. Values
21. Practical
22. Yourself
27. Race

American History Crossword

ACROSS

3. Thomas Jefferson
6. Russia
8. Gold
11. Nebraska
13. United Nations
15. Labor
18. Stock market
19. Kite
20. Monopolies
21. Civil
22. Andrew Jackson

DOWN

1. Louisiana
2. Monroe
4. Erie
5. Abraham Lincoln
7. Panama
9. Franklin Roosevelt
10. F. Scott Key
12. Tom Thumb
14. Spanish-American
16. Democrat
17. Ford
18. Steamboat

Geography Crossword

ACROSS

1. Province
3. Inlet
4. Montreal
5. Concentric circles
6. Commune
7. Tuscany

11. Peak
12. Two hundred
14. Bali
16. Africa
18. Sabang
23. Waterfall
24. Syria
26. Virginia

ACROSS (cont.)
29. Great Whale

DOWN

1. Principality
2. Zagros
4. Margus
6. Cape Krio
8. Appalachian
9. Industrial
10. Burma
13. Damascus

30. Village
31. Nigeria

15. Island
16. Alaska
17. Egypt
19. Bombay
20. Urban
21. Colorado
22. Trengganu
25. Irregular
27. Green
28. Swamp

Home Economics Crossword I: Cooking

ACROSS

2. Quiche Lorraine
5. Paella
6. Skewer
8. Puree
9. Crepes
11. Yeast
12. Mustard
14. Spanikópita
16. Gelatin
17. Grape leaves
20. Scallions
21. Worcestershire

DOWN

1. Currants
3. Chopsticks
4. Ginger root
7. Mezze
10. Braise
12. Marinate
13. Cayenne
15. Whisk
18. Nabemono
19. Cornstarch
20. Samosas

Home Economics Crossword II: Sewing

ACROSS

3. Needle threader
4. Color ball
5. Cross grains
9. Hemstitching
12. Pleats
13. Natural
15. Baste
19. Skirt marker
20. Bodkin
21. Tuck
22. Sharp-point

DOWN

1. French curve
2. Underlining
6. Sleeve board
7. Pin cushion
8. Zigzag
10. Tailor tacker
11. Binding
14. Bias
16. Separating
17. Bobbins
18. Smocking

Industrial Arts Crossword I

ACROSS

1. Spindle molder
5. Varnish
7. Sequoia
8. Knot
10. Taper
13. Yellow pine
15. Unfinished
17. Stop
18. Warp
19. Boats
22. Pitch pine
23. Dowling
25. Cambium
26. Bark
27. Chamfering
29. Jointer
30. Split
31. Sanding
32. Walnut
33. Planer

DOWN

1. Splitting
2. Mahogany
3. Router
4. Jack plane
6. Annual
9. Toenailing
10. Teak
11. Cypress
12. Canary
14. Milk
16. Spruce
19. Bevel
20. Check
21. Pith
24. Oak
27. Carving
28. Filing
31. Stain
32. With

Industrial Arts Crossword II

ACROSS

1. Black ironwood
3. Width
4. Join
5. Wood
8. Barefaced
10. Slide
13. Band saw
14. Jig
15. Sapele
16. Miter
17. Guards
18. Saber saw
20. Keyhole saw
22. Douglas fir
23. Gullets

DOWN

1. Brazil
2. Downward
6. Drift
7. Oxalic acid
9. Dowels
11. Pokerwork
12. Circular
13. Balsa
17. Glue
19. Portable
20. Kerf
21. Jointer
22. Depth

Mathematics Crossword I

ACROSS

3. Much greater than
5. Direction
6. Union
7. Byte
9. Proof
10. Vibration
12. Angle
13. Much less
15. Elimination
17. Root
19. Packing
22. Inertial mass
23. Disjunction

DOWN

1. Identity
2. Conjunction
4. Hyperbolic
8. Parallel to
9. Plane
11. Empty
14. Energy
16. Approaches
18. Dividend
20. Base
21. Divides

Mathematics Crossword II

ACROSS

2. Astronomy
5. Whole
6. Stones
7. Approximations
9. Addend
10. Radius
11. Infinity
12. Longitude
13. Numbers
14. Rectangle
17. Estimate
20. Perimeter
21. Sinh

DOWN

1. Symmetrical
3. Circular wavenumber
4. Rhombohedron
8. Mil
15. Mercator's
16. Counting
18. Lemma
19. Zero

Microcomputers Crossword I

ACROSS

1. Connective
3. Boot
5. Microcomputer
8. Records
10. Stack
12. Chronological
13. Pack

16. Cathode ray tube
17. Step
19. Byte
22. Telephone
24. Ultraviolet
25. Data
26. Subset

DOWN

1. Command
2. Not-and
4. Job
6. Operation
7. Remove
9. Software

11. Flowchart
14. Malfunction
15. Character
18. Receive only
19. Bit
20. Algebra
21. Locations
23. Toggle

Microcomputers Crossword II

ACROSS

1. Screen
3. Records
6. Multiprogramming
8. Editor
11. Kilo
12. Contact
13. Negation
17. Reads
19. Copper
20. Hex
21. Queue
23. Binary
26. Retrieval
27. Digital
28. Index register
29. Conductors
30. Processor

DOWN

1. Semiconductor crystal
2. Program
4. Random-access memory
5. Erases
7. Eight
9. Data cell
10. Terminal
14. And element
15. Overflow
16. Addition
18. Segment
22. Instructions
24. Million
25. Silicon

Music Crossword I: Instruments

ACROSS

3. Bass Clarinet
7. Tambourine
8. Marimba
9. Harp
10. Gong
12. Violoncello
13. Virginal
14. Spinet
16. Piano
17. Kettledrum
21. Mandolin
23. Clavier
24. Trombone

DOWN

1. Tuba
2. Bass
4. ContraBassoon
5. Celesta
6. Cymbal
10. Glockenspiel
11. Concertina
15. Euphonium
18. Clarinet
19. Ukulele
20. Snare
22. Lyre

Music Crossword II

ACROSS

2. Similar
4. A cappella
6. Soft
7. Boat
10. Madrigal
11. Fantasy
12. Forte
15. Majestic
18. Pizzicato
19. Morendo
20. Ornament
23. Dolce
25. Poco
29. Una corda
31. Dolente
32. Staccato
34. Stem
35. Harpsichord

DOWN

1. Sarabande
2. Sad
3. Ritardando
5. Adagio
7. Bravura
8. Duet
9. Very
13. Zither
14. Mezzo
16. Opus
17. Discord
21. Two
22. Operetta
24. Location
26. Kettledrum
27. Glissando
28. Piano
30. All
33. Cymbal

Physical Education Crossword I

ACROSS

2. Olympic games
6. Center
8. Counterattack
12. Backhand
13. Basketball
16. Methanol
18. Goal line
19. Steeplechase
20. Intercept
22. Billiards
23. Scuba diving

DOWN

1. Mountain climbing
3. Pallino
4. Penalty
5. Target
7. Foul
9. Knockout
10. Liquid
11. Draw
14. Kayak
15. Lawn bowling
17. Reel
19. Shoe
21. Cycling

Physical Education Crossword II: Sports

ACROSS

1. Rectangular
4. Zero
7. Harrier
9. Welterweight
11. Center ice
15. Football
16. Seven
17. Lift
20. Yachting
22. Speed
23. Rush
25. Snooker
26. Wickets
30. Ice hockey
32. Ten
34. Duckpin
35. Surfboard

DOWN

1. Rugby
2. Croquet
3. Felt
5. Olympics
6. Three
8. Eighteen
10. Softball
11. Calisthenics
12. Homer
13. Laminated
14. England
18. Tennis
19. Disqualification
21. Ten
22. Skiing
24. Horse
27. Karate
28. Stones
29. Dropkick
31. Kayak
33. Muff

Science Crossword I: Aquariums

ACROSS

1. Skin infections
5. Zeocarb
6. Sand
7. Mixing
9. Cement
10. Stratification
14. Molds
16. Algae
21. Light
22. Overfeeding
25. Water
26. Aeration

DOWN

2. Integument
3. Chlorine
4. Siphon
8. Parasite
11. Fish meal
12. Conditioning
13. Oxygen
15. Light
17. Feeding
18. P. fluorescens
19. Slate
20. Africa
23. Daphnia
24. Salts

Science Crossword II

ACROSS

3. Direct current
6. Opening
7. Right
9. Igneous rock
10. Hygrometer
11. Stars
12. Micrometer
14. Cyclotron
17. Microscope
18. Coil
19. Solidify
21. Parallax
23. Powder
24. Sugar
25. Fusing

DOWN

1. Sidereal year
2. Red
4. Magnification
5. Free
6. Order
8. Food
10. Hydrolysis
13. Monsoon
15. Coal tar
16. Refraction
17. Mesoderm
20. Water
22. Brain

Index